POOR KIDS

1967

A Report on Children in Poverty

POOR

KIDS

Alvin L. Schorr

BASIC BOOKS, INC., PUBLISHERS
New York / *London*

FOR JESSICA, MY DAUGHTER,

in whom daily I see precious qualities that are built on adequacy—energy, boundless curiosity, and compassion. She lacks mainly a world in which all children are favored as she is. This study is an effort to help her have it.

Acknowledgments

Many of the ideas presented in this book were developed while I was working for the Social Security Administration. My colleagues provided a keen and critical climate in which to test ideas. Anyone who has had the good fortune to share the development of ideas with colleagues who are patient, stubborn, and disdainful by turns but always involved and competent, will understand that it is not clear who originates every idea. My colleagues at that time were Mollie Orshansky, Moses Lukaczer, Phillips Cutright, Joseph Bonin, and Johnnie Daniel. Several distinguished demographers lent invaluable counsel, in particular to the preparation of Chapter 5. They were Vincent Whitney, Irene Taeuber, Ronald Freedman, Arthur Campbell, and Nathan Keyfitz.

For one reason and another, many people read parts of my manuscript. I am in the debt of many of them for pointing out some error or suggesting an improvement. Eveline Burns, Beth and Karl de Schweinitz, Martin Rein, and Genevieve Carter took the trouble to comment in detail on the entire manuscript—an act of purest charity having nothing to do with their ordinary obligations. As in many charitable relationships, the recipient has not had the good grace to accept every bit of advice. Even so, what appears in print is much improved by their generous and wise suggestions. Karen Cutright assisted in the preparation of the manuscript—with great good will

Acknowledgments

and the comforting conviction that it should, in its details, reflect the serious purposes that went into writing it.

Chapters 3 and 5 originally appeared, with minor differences, in the *Social Security Bulletin*, issues of February 1966 and December 1965. The excerpt from an article by James Tobin in Appendix IV is reprinted with his permission and the permission of the American Academy of Arts and Sciences. It appeared in *Daedalus*, Vol. 94, No. 4.

How is it possible adequately to thank one's family for the understanding with which they accept the absence and abstraction that are necessary to complete a project such as this?

A. L. S.

CONTENTS

A portfolio of photographs follows page 22.

POOR KIDS

1

Introduction

✝✝✝✝✝✝✝✝✝✝✝✝✝✝✝✝✝✝✝✝✝✝

Our task of reconstruction does not require the creation of new and strange values. It is rather the finding of the way once more to known, but to some degree forgotten, ideals and values. If the means and details are in some instances new, the objectives are as permanent as human nature.

Among our objectives I place the security of the men, women, and children of the Nation first.

—THE PRESIDENT'S MESSAGE TO
CONGRESS, JUNE 8, 1934

The one almost all-embracing measure of security is an assured income . . . in childhood, youth, middle age or old age —in sickness and in health.

—REPORT TO THE PRESIDENT BY
THE COMMITTEE ON ECONOMIC
SECURITY, JANUARY 15, 1935

In 1935 the President's Committee on Economic Security could not have foreseen the magnitude of the developments of the next two or three decades—the wars, the wealth, the technological and social changes. Nevertheless, with remarkable restraint, in only fifty pages, it designed a structure for social security that still stands. The President's Committee be-

3

lieved that the "core" of their planning was for children. Though practical considerations seemed to dictate a piecemeal approach to social security, they intended to assure an income to everyone, including children. In this, as we shall see, they did not succeed.

The broad dimensions of poverty have become well known in the 1960's. In this small book, we are concerned particularly with the children who are poor, poor kids. Our task is to develop a solution to their problem. We shall pursue that task in the spirit of the Committee on Economic Security, placing children at the center of our vision, with the aim of assuring them an income.

Solutions may be approached in various ways, and our results, to some extent, will be influenced by the methods we use. Chapters 2 through 5 deal with the families in which children live. In the first chapter we review the situation of poor children and the reasons why so many are poor. Although most children live in families and income data are given as family incomes, the deliberate focusing on children produces a somewhat different emphasis. The chapter will make it plain that large numbers of children are poor and that we cannot rely on natural processes alone to solve their problem.

Chapter 2 is meant to be a sobering and even challenging statement of the problem of poor children, but those familiar with the literature of poverty will find it conventional. The third chapter pursues an income maintenance program for children through terrain that is largely uncharted. It attempts to describe the relationship of income to children's lives in order to provide a basis for judging various proposed programs of income maintenance. Which children would a given program sustain and how well? Would it enhance their power to make choices? Most statistical data lend themselves to cross-sectional descriptions of people at a single moment in time. Such descriptions provide an anatomy of income but not a physiology of income development. They also frequently fail to distinguish the groups that combine to make an average. Although to attempt a description over time is risky, we

4

will set forth the theory that family and income are not two lines of development, but one, and that the nature and manner of occupational and family choices determine whether or not a poor family will be able to improve its circumstances.

Even if the theory should fail to be convincing, the way in which we arrive at it sets a new requirement. The first question about an income maintenance program should be whether it will meet needs, and we are accustomed to thinking next of economic and fiscal issues. However, economic and fiscal judgments are scanty in this book, in part because they are available elsewhere.* More important, devoting so much space to family and income development involves the view that next in importance to the stark meeting of needs is how the program fits into children's lives. This view is the central point of this book, although it is both difficult and expensive to design a program that takes optimal account of family and income development.

It is necessary to deal in advance with two further aspects of family development, lest issues arise later for which we have no point of view to fall back on. First is the question whether and under what circumstances women should work; the answers have undergone a good deal of change since the depression. This issue overlaps with a larger problem—namely, whether income maintenance affects the willingness to work in general. Chapter 4 attempts to set forth the available research on these issues and to develop a standpoint for public policy. Second, the question is frequently raised as to whether income maintenance programs will increase the overall birth rate or that of any specific group. Chapter 5 reviews the pertinent evidence and concludes that an income maintenance program would not have a detectable effect on birth rates.

Chapters 6 through 9 turn to income maintenance. Chapter 6 sets forth guidelines for evaluating income maintenance pro-

* Two comprehensive discussions of issues in developing social security are *Nation and Family*[131] and *Social Security and Public Policy*.[21]

grams. We propose an honest if not a neutral study of the possibilities. That we must have an open society in which children may seek and achieve at least a measure of equality may be a debatable proposition in some quarters, but not here. The notion is presented that a program must, besides assuring the delivery of goods and services to children, fit into their lives in a manner that opens choices to them: where to live, how to live, at what to work. This may sound painfully general, but the reader will judge whether it affects our appraisal of the issues.

The sixth chapter examines alternative remedies for childhood poverty. Programs that open up job opportunities may merit further exploration in relation to children. On the other hand, children's needs might best be met by furnishing them outright with housing, food, and clothing. Even if one insists upon cash programs, it is possible to improve public assistance or to replace existing income maintenance programs with a new, broader, unified program. Each of these points of view may suggest an alternative line of action or at least a course of study. Our choice is to attempt to devise a new cash payment program focused upon children.

Chapters 7 through 9 deal with the program proposals that the earlier chapters prepared for. The historic course of social security has been to identify a major risk that may produce need and to devise a category for it. The risk (retirement, unemployment) becomes the center of attention, and administration of assistance follows the pattern of other social security programs. We shall entertain a proposal of this sort: fatherless child insurance, to protect against the risk of family breakdown. If we concentrate on the fact of need itself, the resultant program will revolve about the definition of need and the method of administration. The negative income tax (NEGIT), to which Chapter 8 is devoted, is such a program. A final and somewhat different approach is the demogrant— "typically a payment made to all persons above or below a certain age, with no other eligibility conditions . . ." [22] The relevant possibility is a program of family allowances.

It should be said at once that no particular program will, in the end, be anointed. Our purpose is rather to establish the boundaries of feasibility so that if one program is rejected, another may be chosen. Those who will may play the game of detecting biases or personal preferences in the discussion that follows, but these are not central.

A few cautionary notes: Statistics seem to lead increasingly transient lives; the numbers of children who are poor, the numbers in broken families, and so forth change with each new survey. The numbers used here are as accurate as scholarship can make them; but our interest lies in relationships, in magnitudes, and in trends that persist while the numbers they encompass change. Second, organizational issues in relation to income maintenance programs are not treated at all. Obviously the question of what agency of government would operate a program has a bearing on efficiency and public acceptance, but the purpose has to be settled first. Tables of organization do not make an apt program any more than lines drawn to perspective make a Buffet. Finally, a number of terms will be used that are more broadly or ambiguously used in public discussion. Some of them can quite properly be used otherwise than as defined here. We define them in relation to one another, however, in order to promote a coherent discussion.

I

CHILDREN AND FAMILIES

✝✝✝✝✝✝✝✝✝✝✝✝✝✝✝✝✝✝✝✝

2

... And Children
of the
Nation First

✝✝✝✝✝✝✝✝✝✝✝✝✝✝✝✝✝✝✝✝✝

In 1963, of the 69 million children in
the United States who lived in families, 15.6 million were poor.*
Depending upon one's definition of poverty, the number of

---

* Data in this chapter not otherwise attributed were provided by the Social Security Administration from studies under the direction of Mollie Orshansky. Published reports are "Children of the Poor," [136] "Counting the Poor: Another Look at the Poverty Profile," [138] and "Who's Who among the Poor." [139]

poor children can be enlarged or diminished.* It may be well, therefore, to be explicit about what this particular figure means. The portion of income that a family uses for food may be regarded as a rough indicator of its prosperity. That is, as total income goes up, a smaller and smaller percentage is devoted to food. The poorest families spend a third or more of their income on food; other families generally spend a smaller proportion. The point at which total income is less than three times the cost of the basic nutritional requirements of a family (of specified size and ages) may be viewed as the brink of poverty. Basic requirements are determined here—some will think too stringently—by the economy food plan developed by the Department of Agriculture. The economy food plan is for "temporary or emergency use when funds are low." In the long run it cannot provide an adequate diet. It is by this standard that almost one fourth of the children in the United States are counted as poor.

These are the primitive elements of a standard of living: food, clothing, shelter, and medical care. How do American children make out in these simplest terms? Even poor families find defenses against lack of food. If total income is inadequate, food costs may be met first (along with rent and utilities) and other needs sacrificed. Mothers may starve themselves in order to feed their children adequately.[233] A series of studies makes it clear, nevertheless, that inadequate diet follows upon inadequate income. For example, a Cleveland study of 100 families with 446 children traced the following results to "low income . . . only": two thirds of the families had substantial deficits of two or more basic nutrients (calcium, vitamins A or C); most of the teenagers might count on only one cup of milk a day; half the families had only one serving of fruit or vegetables a day—or none.[31]

About the extent to which children are inadequately clothed,

* Other definitions are found in *The Annual Report of the Council of Economic Advisers*,[48] *Income and Welfare in the United States*,[128] and *Poverty and Deprivation in the United States*.[35]

comparatively little is known. From time to time one reads about children kept out of school for lack of clothes,* but scientific precision would require that we know how many. Quite possibly clothing of sound quality has become comparatively easy to come by and the least acute of the deficits that poor children suffer. Rather more is known about the housing of children. In 1960 about 10 million children lived in houses that lacked a proper toilet, bath, or hot water. About 4 million lived in housing that census enumerators called dangerous.[201]

As for medical care, the President's Task Force on Manpower Conservation estimates that one third of all youths turning eighteen are unqualified for induction into the Armed Forces. The majority of rejectees "appear to be victims of inadequate education and insufficient health services." [145] The Task Force report suggests that children's poverty and poor health reinforce each other; the National Health Survey substantiates this. Telephone consultations between parents and physicians are common when children are ill. The average child in families with an annual income over $4,000 was the subject of one or more such consultations a year; among families with less than $2,000, fewer than one child in five benefited from a telephone consultation in a given year. Similarly, poorer children averaged fewer visits to a doctor's or dentist's office. A child in a family with over $4,000 in annual income is almost twice as likely as a poorer child to have visited a dentist. Three out of four of the poorer children have never seen a dentist.[207, 164]

Mention must be made of the tangible effects of poverty on the family in which a child lives. Although the precise relationship of family breakdown and poverty is debatable, it is clear that poor families suffer more.[28] Of the children counted as poor, one out of three lives in a family without a father—as compared with one out of twenty-three children not counted as poor who

* "There still are hundreds of children in the Nation's Capital who go to school 'without a bite' or don't go to school because they are without shoes." [49]

13

live in such a family. Six hundred thousand poor children escape "poverty by living . . . with relatives whose combined income is adequate for all." [138] Teenagers apparently spin off from their families—because nothing keeps them or perhaps because they are a burden. At any rate, there are fewer teenagers in poor families than seems reasonable in relation to the number of younger children. Uncounted young children have been given up entirely by their families for primarily financial reasons and drift from home to home or enter the care of social agencies. [114, 44, 49, 56]

It is apparent that the 15.6 million children about whom we are concerned make out badly by the most primitive standards. It should not be supposed that the scales are balanced in other ways. A bit of modern folklore surrounds the prevalence of television sets in poor homes. Certainly television is widely regarded as a necessity. For example, a sociologist asked parents in desperate circumstances how they managed to have television. One had had her telephone removed but kept the television set. "You can count on TV any old time," she said, "but if you want to talk to somebody on the phone he's got to be there." A father of five sold most of his furniture but kept the bed, chairs, and television set. He said "he felt he should have kept [the books] for his children but decided that it was more important for them to have TV." [99] Nevertheless, probably a third of poor children are without television. [198]

The reasons why poor children are even more severely deprived of recreation, personal care, and so forth hardly need mention. First, if food and shelter use up all the money, none is left. Second, not enough money makes for wasteful management. Purchases are made in dribbles, or on credit which costs more in the long run, and evictions and repossessions pile new costs upon others. Third, those who suffer from malnutrition and inadequate housing have physiological cause for managing poorly. Technical data are available on the manner in which health and competence are affected. [169, 167, 182] A bit of personal testimony will make the point. Having lived his years in the desert of hunger and homelessness, George Orwell wrote in 1933:

> Hunger reduces one to an utterly spineless, brainless condition, more like the aftereffects of influenza than anything else . . . Complete inertia is my chief memory of hunger.[140]

We have dealt so far largely with the commodities that poor children lack. Another cost of poverty to children is that they live among poor people, whether on the farm, in the heart of the city, or in suburban enclaves. Characteristically these areas are poorer in public services. The free public schools are not so well supported. Their teachers are not so well trained and come and go more frequently. The supply of physicians and dentists is comparatively low, for they locate where paying patients are to be found and where they can themselves benefit from good public services. And voluntary agencies, if they have been established at all, have difficulty in raising funds in poor communities. Their finances may keep pace with rising costs but not with growing needs or a growing clientele. Thus, poor children are deprived not only by lack of income but by lack of access to services meant to be universal.

In short, poor children in the United States are poorly sheltered, many of them do not eat adequately, and their medical care is insufficient. Their right to an intact family is compromised. Their recreational and personal needs are not met. They do not even benefit from proper education. It would be hardly worth saying these things if we could bear to keep them in mind. The children suffering from each of these deficiencies must be numbered in the millions. On the average, families with poor children have about three fifths of the income required to escape poverty. How does one account for such deprivation among children today—thirty years after the report of the Committee on Economic Security—in a land overflowing with prosperity?

15

SOURCES OF CHILDHOOD POVERTY

For the moment, we shall speak of the sources of poverty superficially, noting employment and unemployment but not asking why a man failed in competition with other men, noting family breakdown but not asking why this particular family was affected. Poor children may be classified roughly into three groups —one third live in homes headed by men who have regular work, one third in the homes of men who do not, and one third in homes headed by women.

Most poor children live in a home headed by a man. For these families work would unequivocally seem to be the route to a decent income. But in 1963, 1.5 million families with a father regularly employed were poor; they included 5.2 million children. Thus responsibility for a third of the children who are poor must be charged to employment that does not, even with full time devoted to it, provide an income adequate to family needs. The problem of minimum income is compound. On one hand, it is a problem of the poorly paid occupations—laborer, farmer, and so forth. On the other hand, a modest income of, say, $4,000 does not, for urban families of six or more, escape the standard we have described as poverty. Unfortunately men who work in poorly paid occupations tend, generally speaking, to have larger families.

In 1963 another third of the poor children lived in the families of men who had worked part-time, less than a full year, or not at all. When asked, about two out of five of those who had been continuously unemployed during the year referred to illness or disability. Who is disabled depends, of course, upon how badly workers are wanted. In any case, an unemployment rate that hovers about 4 per cent constitutes an obvious risk of poverty for children. For the unemployed (that is, those able to work and seeking work), the Committee on Economic Security proposed programs of unemployment insurance. However, not everyone is

covered and most state programs provide for at most six months
of benefit payments. Of those unemployed for five weeks or more,
only about half receive unemployment insurance payments.[180]
The average weekly payment is $36 [214]—an amount insufficient to
keep a family with children from being classified as poor.

Four million children, or somewhat less than a third of those
who are poor, live in families headed by women. The income deficit in these families is larger than in those headed by men. On the
average, they have only about half the income required to escape
poverty. Work may constitute an acceptable route to income for
families headed by women but depends on a number of considerations—the age and number of children, availability of child
care, previous training of the mother. In fact, early in 1964 more
than a third of the mothers heading poor families were at work
or seeking work. Children in families without a father thus suffer
to some extent from the same difficulties as families with a father
—low wages and a labor market in which only the best prepared
can count on finding work. Moreover, a husband earning little
may look to his wife to supplement his wages, but a divorced or
widowed woman relies perforce on herself. Even with full employment and a high minimum wage, a substantial number of children
in families headed by women would remain poor.* Some women
could not, would not, or should not leave their children for the
day. The exigencies of children's daily needs limit the types of
work their mothers can do. Women do not, in general, have the
work habits or skills that men do.

Survivors' insurance was intended to provide a floor of income
for children whose fathers died. However, partly because some
fathers have not achieved coverage under social security, survivors' insurance is currently paid to only about 70 per cent of pa-
ternal orphans. Of those who do receive payments, almost a third
(550,000 children) must nevertheless be counted as poor—a re-

* With a minimum wage of $1.40 an hour, income from forty hours of work a
week would not exceed the poverty level for a family of four.

flection on the amounts of payments.[210] Aid to Families with Dependent Children (AFDC) was also intended to meet the needs of children without fathers, whether orphaned or not. However, only about 40 to 50 per cent of such poor children receive AFDC at any given moment; and payments are made in such low amounts[129] that most children receiving aid would be counted as poor anyway.

We have now totted up the children who are poor and the programs that were meant to succor them. Obviously the need for a vigorous peace-time economy with high wages and full employment is at the heart of the matter. Diligence and wisdom are being invested to develop the necessary techniques, and we propose no contribution in this area. But time passes for children while we are achieving the objectives we do visualize. For these casualties of (what is the clinical euphemism?) frictional unemployment and of the crude economic techniques of the moment, for children without a father, and for children poor for miscellaneous reasons, a variety of income maintenance programs is required. But if we are not without resources of this sort—and we are not—why do current programs fall short by 15.6 million children?

We have observed about each of the relevant programs that it reaches only half to three fourths of the children for whom it is specifically designed. Moreover, payments are not high enough to preclude poverty for the children reached. Unfortunately this problem does not arise merely from an oversight. Public assistance incurs a set of problems we shall discuss later. The other programs are social insurance programs, with benefits roughly related to contributions that were, when they were made, based on income. Benefits are not generally planned to replace all income; in principle, other resources will also be available. To make a minimum benefit high enough to eliminate poverty among beneficiaries would, if other payments were scaled upward in accordance with the insurance principle, entail an extremely expensive program. The dilemma has been resolved by compromise, by providing formulas for calculating benefits that give some advantage to those who are poor but not sufficient advantage to eradicate poverty.

For example, about half of those unemployed receive no unemployment insurance at all.[214] Studies show that these are families whose incomes were lower to begin with[32, 224] and which are more likely to contain children. Similarly, families with a father who earned little receive the lowest survivors' benefits. Savings and other private resources are most likely to be available to those whose incomes were higher and who now receive higher benefits. Thus the advantage on one side and disadvantage on the other are compounded, and the compromise between insurance and meeting need has an effect in no way intended. This effect has been put as follows by Robert Lampman:

> Our system of income maintenance, which now pays out $35 billion in benefits per year, is aimed more at the problem of income insecurity of the middle class and at blocking returns to poverty than in facilitating exits from poverty for those who have never been out of poverty.[102]

The discussion so far echoes the conventional American (one is tempted to say, conventional Calvinist) syllogism: Work means income. Unemployment means lack of income. Protect against lack of income by protecting against unemployment. But hidden from view is a striking demographic fact—namely, that three out of four poor youths can make one or both of these statements: "I did not live with my father or even a man I could call father"; and "My family has five or more children." * Thus

---

* In 1963, 63 per cent of poor children answered these descriptions. Obviously some who currently lacked a father more usually had a father. On the other hand, some counted in families headed by men were to lose their father. It is assumed that these two types of changes balance each other. Some children currently in smaller families had brothers and sisters already adult or would have

19

most poor children are readily described in terms of social risk; they are vulnerable to low income because of a family character-istic. (Possibly the risks we accept are regarded as economic and those we do not yet accept are called social.) From the point of view of these three out of four children, current programs fail to meet their needs because major risks to them are not even in prin-ciple covered. In truth, either the economic or the social explana-tion, taken independently, is oversimple. We shall see how closely interwoven are large families, broken families, and poor earning ability.

That three out of four poor children belong to one or an-other of these poverty-vulnerable family types means that we can-not rely solely on the healing processes of a vigorous economy. If one overlooks the problem of the moment (the moment that is a lifetime for some children), rising wage levels and concomitant improvement of the social insurances can be expected steadily to reduce the number of children who are poor. On the other hand, the number of children in poverty-vulnerable families is on the rise.

Fundamental shifts in American patterns of marriage and birth are involved in the increase in vulnerable children. Young men and women are marrying earlier and having children earlier. In 1959, men were two years younger when first married and at the birth of their first child than in 1940; women were 1.3 years younger.[73] If children are born earlier in marriage, more children are likely to be caught in their parents' divorce. In fact, the num-ber so caught has been rising steadily and now approaches half a million a year.[208] About three fourths of divorced men remarry; the rate is higher among younger men. For this and other reasons,

new brothers and sisters. Therefore, the percentage of youths who can lay claim to the two statements cited is higher than the 63 per cent of whom they are true at a given moment. The corresponding percentage for children who were not poor in 1963 was 13 per cent. (These percentages are derived from "Counting the Poor." [138])

support payments are not easy to procure upon divorce.[10, 94, 17] Thus the children of divorce are increasing in number, but the money available to them is limited.

Official figures account for only legal divorce, but informal family breakdown is increasing in the same way. The number of mothers with low income (under $2,000 a year), without a man in the home, and still of child-bearing age (under thirty-five) increased by one fifth between 1949 and 1959. In other words, the number of young, husbandless mothers with less than $2,000 income increased; yet $2,000 was worth less at the end of the ten-year period.[8] Mothers without husbands generally have more children in their lifetime than mothers with husbands; thus the disadvantage that accrues to large families is added to their burden.

It may be worth recognizing that socially orphaned children —children of divorce and separation—are a product of widely approved, basic American values. We are very much a marrying and a child-bearing people. We seem to be unaware that people have lived satisfying lives without a mate and a child. We also require that love be personally satisfying. When it does not turn out that way, we divorce or separate and try again if we can. Former generations did not know even as luxuries the things we regard as necessities. To obtain the things we must have we move, with pain sometimes but without a real alternative, in search of jobs or better jobs. In the ensuing movement and change, we experience satisfaction, but also shock and maladjustment. When we do not achieve our objectives, we feel unmanned or unfeminine and unvalued.

This set of values gives to many children homes in which they are cherished and surrounded by material possessions. It is fundamentally the same set of values that leaves other children with no father. Socially orphaned children are the casualties of a family pattern oriented to quality of relationship, to happiness, and to material possessions, just as cherished children are its successes. To understand this is to understand a phenomenon that

2 1

may be controlled but is not likely to be rooted out. Family breakdown may continue to increase; there is no sign on the horizon that it is likely to decline.

We can now sum up the sources of childhood poverty. Work does not pay enough. There is not enough full-time work for all; or, as some prefer to say, not everyone has the capacity and training to command full-time work. The programs we have established do not protect all the children they set out to protect. For the children protected, benefit levels are frequently not high enough to avoid poverty. Many children are deprived of a father and many live in families too large for their income. Against these two contingencies that handicap three out of four poor children we do not have a program of social insurance, even in principle.

Numbers and generalizations inevitably lack immediacy. It may help to let a handful of visible children stand proxy for the 15 or 16 million.

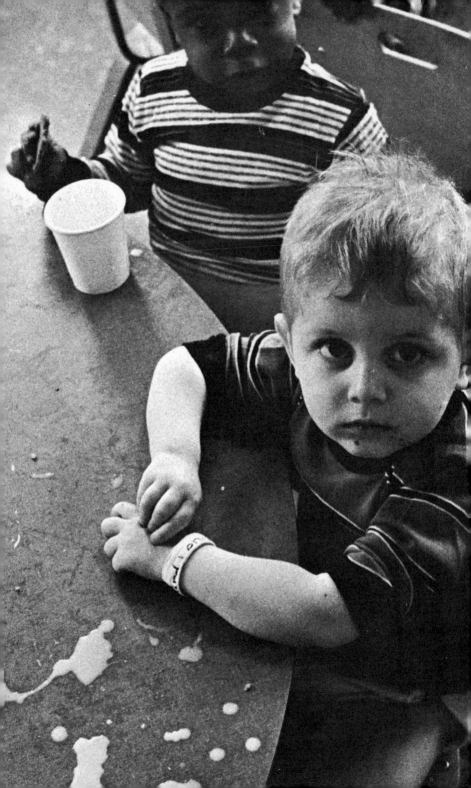

*They are black and white, sick, hungry, crowded, in families,
in the streets, in the country. It is their question we answer.*

3

The Family
Cycle
and Income
Development

✝✝✝✝✝✝✝✝✝✝✝✝✝✝✝✝✝✝✝✝

It is generally true that most people who die poor were born poor. It is also partially true that poor people reveal typical attitudes and behavior and teach them to their children. Human manipulation has made from these observations a nonfact or artifact: the poor are said to move about in a self-contained aura of attitudes that are more or less independent of their life experience; the attitudes themselves produce their poverty. It would be hard to imagine a more comfortable mystique for those who are not poor. It is less flattering and more taxing to the mind to grasp the back-and-forth play between facts of life and attitudes toward life, between what seems practical and what one aspires to. Yet this is our task if we are to understand how an income maintenance program may influence its beneficiaries.

Some light might be shed on the mystique of the "culture of poverty" by a simple examination of the effect of poor food or poor housing on behavior. Ample evidence testifies to the capacity of such deficiences to produce the attitudes associated with poor people.[169, 167, 182] Orwell, participant-observed when he was hungry, might have seemed typically culturally poor. However, it will better serve our purpose to take another approach and attempt to relate the stages through which a family passes to the development of family income. It is the progress of a child from poverty to adequacy that we seek to achieve, and it is a family of some sort that will receive income from any program we devise.

Available studies and statistics are poorly adaptable to an outline of the family-income cycle. We may simplify our problem by including only poor families, but even then no one knows whether there are one, two, or several typical modes of development. It is clear only that not every family now poor necessarily started out poor or will end poor. In order to attempt to discern a pattern, we shall identify overlapping and partially sequential stages in family life. We shall prepare no surprises. The stages are selected because they represent crises on two planes at once—family development and income development. If the wrong choice, in terms of future income, is made at the first stage, the right choice becomes progressively harder to make at each subsequent stage. The four stages are these: (1) timing and circumstances of first marriage or child-bearing; (2) timing and direction of occupational choice; (3) family cycle squeeze—the conflict of aspiration and need; and (4) family breakdown.

INITIAL MARRIAGE AND CHILD-BEARING

Women who married for the first time in 1960 were, on the average, about twenty years old. By twenty-seven or twenty-eight, the median wife will have had her last child.[73] Within a general trend to young marriage and child-bearing, it appears that the very youngest will have lower incomes and less stable families. Although the evidence comes from studies that are variously focused,* it is wholly consistent. For example, "youthful marriages are less satisfactory to the participants and less stable than marriages contracted by persons who are out of their teens." [19] The incidence of poverty among families with heads fourteen to twenty-four years old, already high by the end of World War II, had increased by 1960. "The honor of being called family head, bestowed too soon," observes Oscar Ornati, "brings with it a greater likelihood of poverty." [134] This observation refers only to the relationship of early marriage to income shortly after marriage.

That the relationship of early marriage to low income persists over time can be seen in Table 3–1. Education and occupation are both substantial indications of income. The husbands of wives who first married younger than seventeen are far more likely than other husbands, twenty years later or more, to have the poorest education and work. Their chances of turning up with

---

* It is also of varying vintage. Arguing forty years ago that we were moving toward a norm in which eighteen would be the youngest age at which girls would marry, Mary Richmond and Fred Hall observed: "The daughter who in the Old Country would have been married at the first chance, must now, for a few years at least, delay marriage—often will wish to do so—in order to help in putting her own and her family's fortunes on a firmer foundation." [154]

25

TABLE 3–1. *Education and Occupation of Husband by Age When Wife Was First Married, for Families in Which the Wife Was Thirty-five Years Old or More in 1960*

		EDUCATION OF HUSBAND		OCCUPATION OF HUSBAND	
AGE OF WIFE AT FIRST MARRIAGE	PER CENT OF TOTAL NUMBER OF FAMILIES	PER CENT WITH 11 YEARS OF SCHOOL OR LESS	PER CENT WITH 13 YEARS OR MORE	PER CENT OPERATIVES, SERVICE, OR LABORERS	PER CENT PROFESSIONAL OR TECHNICAL OR MANAGERIAL OFFICIALS
14 to 16	8	83	4	44	12
17 and 18	15	76	6	38	16
19 and 20	19	67	13	32	20
21 and 22	17	60	21	29	26

Source: U. S. Census 1960, *Families*, PC(2)4A, Tables 52 and 55.

some college education or a professional or technical job are very small indeed.* Putting together the two cross-sections, one shortly after marriage and the other a decade or two later, we may conclude that low income is likely to be a continual experience for those who marry before eighteen.

Table 3–1 understates the risk in young marriages. It deals with intact marriages and omits those women whose marriages did not last and who had not, by 1960, remarried. The omission

* The age of women at marriage must be permitted to tell the story for their husbands, as the 1960 census distinguished between men who had married younger or older than twenty-two but did not distinguish below that age. Even dealing with that comparatively advanced age, the data suggest the same conclusion. The men who married between twenty-two and twenty-seven eventually hold better jobs than those who married before twenty-two.[198]

One would suppose that low income would result in smaller accumulation of goods or savings. *Income and Welfare in the United States*[128] observes: "The data seem to confirm the hypothesis that early arrival of children is associated with less accumulation of capital by the family, even when adjustments are made for differences in age, education, inheritances, and unemployment experiences."

is consequential, for the evidence is also clear that earlier marriages tend to be less stable. If they married before seventeen, for example, three out of ten women between twenty-five and thirty-four have remarried or their husbands have remarried. Only a fraction more than one out of ten who first married at twenty, however, have remarried by the same ages.[198] Paul Glick has observed that, after a lapse of thirty years, only half of the women married by seventeen are still living with the first husband.[72]

Although these statistics are clear about the risks to income and stability in young marriages, they do not begin to explain them. To understand the statistics, it is necessary to gain some background. A substantial number of children (perhaps 20 per cent of all legitimate first children) are conceived before marriage.[29, 30] From this we do not conclude, as once we might have, that one out of five marriages was forced. Rather it appears that many young people who are planning to be married simply anticipate the ceremony. The situation is rather different among those who marry at sixteen or seventeen. The girl and quite possibly the boy have not finished school. Even if they contemplated marriage, all sorts of practical difficulties would deter them. In fact, the percentage of premarital conceptions among youths is much higher than 20 per cent. Studies in a variety of localities reveal premarital pregnancy rates that range upward from one third of all school-age marriages to 87 per cent where both parties were high school students.[19] We must conclude, then, that many young marriages are indeed forced marriages.

Whether forced or not, young marriages face a number of practical problems. Table 3–1 shows that young marriage is associated with less education for the husband. Of girls dropping out of high school, 40 per cent tell an interviewer that marriage or pregnancy is the reason.[143] In the climate of postwar attitudes, a young husband readily completes his own education, at any rate, while his wife works. If the couple are very young and already have a baby, however, this is harder to accomplish. Education and training are increasingly competitive requirements in a period when many youths are unemployed. Indeed, at any given moment, one of five youths without a high school diploma is unemployed.[89, 186] At least as many drop-outs are probably not even seeking work.[139] Thus the young marriage is likely to start with unemployment compounded, when work turns up, by comparatively low wages.

We have proceeded so far as though all families begin with marriage, and of course they do not. Earlier we noted the prevalence of poverty among families headed by women; obviously mothers who start out without a husband are no better off. Nor do we suppose that pregnancy before marriage or at a young age is the first cause of poverty, which follows as an automatic punishment for transgression. Sometimes causality does move in this direction. For example, a pioneer study raised doubts about simple formulations relating low fertility to self-improvement.* Yet those couples whose incomes actually declined seemed to have been "selected for initial lack of fertility control." [155] At the same time, we know that those who are already uninterested in education may more usually engage in premarital relations or wish to get married at a young age. People's ambitions and efforts to realize them flow together day by day. Whether lack of interest in school leads to marriage or vice versa is knowledge to which only each youngster is privy, if indeed he knows himself.

When a couple starts out together early, they are not only likely to have their first child earlier than usual; they are likely to have more children. White mothers who were married by the age of eighteen average 3.7 children by the time their families are completed and Negro mothers 4.3 children.[202] By contrast, white and Negro mothers married at about twenty-one years of

* The theory of social capillarity, stated in 1890, appears regularly in other metamorphoses. Arsène Dumont's original theory is stated as follows: "Just as a column of liquid has to be thin in order to rise under the force of capillarity, so a family must be small in order to rise in the social scale." *Dépopulation et Civilization* (Paris: 1890), quoted by Charles F. Westoff.[219]

age have 2.8 and 4.0 children respectively. The difference is not simply that the younger couples get a head start. Rather, those who marry young and are fated to be poor tend to have children early and late. The others concentrate their children in a few years and have fewer all told.[202] Is it that poor people want to have more children? It seems not. All evidence suggests that American families, whatever their income, want to have about the same number of children. Those who are poor do not succeed in limiting the number.[155, 64, 63] One study, *Growth of American Families*, puts the matter this way:

> Lower status couples don't have more children . . . simply because they want more. They have more children because some of them do not use contraception regularly and effectively. If the wife has a grade school education and if the husband has an income of less than $3,000 a year, then 39 per cent have excess fertility . . . The judgment that their fertility is too high is their own opinion.[87]

Our point, for the moment, is simply that early marriage sets the stage for a large family. By the rigors of arithmetic alone, more income will be required to escape poverty. The other handicaps that a large family presents to the acquiring of income will be discussed later.

Referring a quarter of a century ago to countless surveys already conducted, Richard and Kathleen Titmuss observed that "children . . . introduce insecurity into the home." [192] Young couples are likely to face the problem of providing for a child quite early. They are likely to face the problem of providing for more than the average number of children. They are likely to face these problems with insufficient training and education. They are more than ordinarily likely to suffer separation or divorce. For a few families with money or otherwise fortunate, early parenthood presents no problem. Others are not barred by early marriage

29

from developing a decent income, but the rules of the game press harder upon them.

OCCUPATIONAL CHOICE

By the time a wage earner reaches his mid-twenties, the limits of his lifetime income have in large measure been established. He will have continued in school or not. The issue is not whether he drops out of school and returns but whether he has left for several years and is unable to return. In the decade before retirement age a man who has completed college earns two thirds more, on the average, than a man who has only completed high school and over twice as much as a man who has only completed grade school.[203] The diploma or degree (or qualities attached to getting it) counts for more than the prorated years of schooling it represents. The college graduate approaching retirement earns over $10,000, but the man of the same age with one to three years of college earns $7,000.

Apart from education, the young adult will have taken his first job and established a pattern of job movement. White-collar and professional workers (and readers) may be given to thinking of jobs in terms of choice. Studies of manual laborers, blue-collar workers, the lower class, or the working class make it clear that their entry into the job market is compounded of accident and immediate necessity. A study of youths doing manual work in 1951 summarized their situations as follows:

> Most youngsters (and their parents) approached the choice of a first job with no clear conception of where they were going; the great majority of first jobs were found in a very informal way, preponderantly through relatives and friends; the great majority of youngsters took the *first job* they found and did not make comparisons with any other job; their knowledge of the job before they took it was in most cases extremely meager; and in

most cases the job turned out to be a blind alley . . . [author's italics].[152]

In 1964 other researchers were still trying to counter "the myth of occupational choice." S. M. Miller wrote that, on the contrary, working-class jobs are "a recurring and frequently unpredictable series of events in which 'choice' is frequently the obverse of necessity."[123] Despite its chance beginning, the first job is an excellent indication of what the last job will be. The first ten years of work—with exceptions, to be sure—foreshadow the rest.[111, 152]

The choices made by people who are going to be poor may seem haphazard, but their combined effect is as accidental as the path of a trolley car. The youth enters upon work unready. He may have left school because he wanted to—whatever that says about his life situation. He may have left school because of sheer financial need. For example, a national study showed that withdrawing public assistance from families who needed it ended the schooling of some of the children.[20] The youth's bargaining power is not good and it is a doubtful favor to tell him otherwise. He knows astonishingly little about the consequences of his choice of job. In terms of immediate payoff, the difference between one job and another may not be great. The long-range payoff is lost to him in scholarly studies and school administrators' offices. In one sense help from parents is nonexistent and in another sense all too available. Although parents tend to want much for their children, they know little about how to prepare for occupations other than their own. The links they can provide are to the work they have known. If one considers the interesting, though speculative, concept that careers proceed according to a timetable learned from others, then it may be possible to say that parents also pass on a handicapping sense of the timetable normally to be followed.[161] That is, they may pass on expectations that start the youth at work too early and lead him to move too slowly or at the wrong times.

We have noted the high unemployment rate among youths; some stay in school only because of the unemployment rate.[14] In the circumstances, those who are out of school believe they do well to seize the first job that is offered. Thinking individually and realistically, who is to gainsay them? All the evidence shows that young people with inadequate education will, in the years to come, increasingly be concentrated among the lowest income groups.[18] Over a third of marriages involve boys twenty-one or younger. Other boys have responsibilities to parents or brothers and sisters and are in no position to refuse even dead-end jobs. As for the rest, any beginning salary may look large compared with what they have had. Nor should we overlook a youth's possible immaturity. The penalties of the choice he is making may be hidden, but its benefits—cash in the pocket, independence, adult status—call to his deepest needs. In this respect higher education holds out a great, if homely, advantage, for vocationally speaking the late teens and early twenties tend to be a "floundering period" anyway.[41, 111] A youngster without advanced education enters upon his career uncertain and immature, while the youngster who spends a period in college evaluates work from the vantage point of four additional years.

By their middle twenties, youths have made other, interlocking decisions that bind them. Women have decided whether or not to work, and in their schooling and job choices they too have bounded the sort of work they may do later. Obviously these decisions influence the family's income, but—equally significant in the long run—women who work will have fewer children.[62] A very small family is not typical of ambitious couples starting out with a decent income, but it is typical of couples starting out with great disadvantages and determined to make their way at all costs.[155] For example, the higher their husband's income, the fewer are the white women who reach menopause without having a child. But the largest percentage of nonwhite childless women are in the $3,000 to $7,000 bracket.[202] Presumably the struggle for nonwhites to attain a modest income is somehow eased by their having no children at all. In nonwhite families with incomes above $7,000 childlessness is not as common as in the moderate income group; apparently $7,000 represents a balance point beyond which a child does not block the family's aspirations.

Young men, women, and couples may also have faced a choice as to whether to move to where jobs are more readily available. Those who do move are less likely to be unemployed.[186] An English study observes that the ages between twenty and thirty are crucial for skilled workers in a depressed area. "Now is taken the vital decision to move or to stay." But before the unskilled "are out of their teens some . . . are almost completely precluded from exercising any free choice in their careers." [174] The evidence in the United States is consistent with this. The highest mobility rate is between twenty and thirty, and the better educated are more likely to have moved.[106] So too larger families are less likely to move.* [63]

We noted that in Stage 1 young marriages run a high risk of dissolution. By the time the couples are in their mid-twenties, the determination of stability or separation is likely to have been made. Separation creates an obvious income problem for the mother and her children. The father has a problem too, unless he can escape it. He is probably liable for support payments which, if they look small to those who complain of growing irresponsibility,

---

* Two examples of families unable to move: "A 26-year-old man with ten years of schooling unloads and washes hogs in a meat packing business. The job is steady, but he is very dissatisfied about the smells of the place and 'the whole set-up'—the smell nauseates him so that he often is unable to eat his lunch. But he has just bought a ramshackle bungalow and cannot afford the risk of changing to another, possibly less secure, job. A 33-year-old man, a bottler in a beer company, struggles to support his wife and three children on $3,000 a year pay. He does not like his job, but he also feels that he cannot risk giving up a secure job." [99]

loom large to the father with a limited income. Whatever the reason, men who have been married only once show steady job improvement during the first decade of marriage. In contrast, the status of men who remarry improves little.[9]

Finally, not only is each job decision important, but the sequence of jobs is also important. Harold Wilensky has carefully elaborated the consequences of an orderly work history, in which "one job normally leads to another, related in function and higher in status." [226, 228, 225] The man who pursues an orderly career shows strong attachment to his work and continues to make progress. The man who shifts about without apparent reason or benefit is likely to be dissatisfied and blocked.

The permutations leading to even key decisions are numerous, but perhaps several useful generalizations may be extracted from these disorderly patterns. First, although occupational and family decisions may be the subject matter of different professional disciplines, as families live they are a unity. The decision to marry and begin work, for example, is more likely to be one decision than two. Second, extreme family types are readily discernible even at this early point. On the one hand are the heroic families—those husbands and wives who stick together (with pleasure or without), overcome their antecedents, study and work and forego children. We cannot assume that all of these families achieve reasonable objectives, but obviously some do. Then there are the families defeated from the beginning—pregnant early, married early, dropped out of school, soon separated, and unlikely to have enough income at any time. In between are most poor families, undoubtedly encompassing two or three or several types. Third, the common problem youths face with regard to school, family, and work, lies in their being forced to make decisions prematurely and unprepared. In the situation in which poor youths find themselves, the alternative to one choice for which they are unprepared (completing school) is another choice for which they are also not ready (early marriage or work). It may be that we require devices to postpone the necessity for any of these choices at seventeen or eighteen or twenty.

Although we have arrived at this conclusion by a narrow consideration of occupational development, a parallel conclusion may be reached by a psychological route. For instance, Erik Erikson argues for a "psychological moratorium—a period of delay in the assumption of adult commitment." [55] Because of the swift changes and shifting values of our times, youths require a period of relaxed expectation, of experimenting with various kinds of work, or even of introspection to locate their sense of adult identity.[53, 54, 156]

Two lines of argument—the occupational and the psychological—unite in the recognition that in our society the major source of social identity for men is work. Lee Rainwater, who has explored this matter, argues that if a sense of identity is blocked by the avenue of work it may be sought instead through expressive behavior—speech, song, actions, or idiosyncratic ideas. Rainwater observes that the expressive solution is only temporarily satisfying to low-income youths;[149] but given time and the opportunity, they may shift to a sense of identity through work. This observation too implies the need for providing time for a youth before he commits himself to a line of work.

As a final generalization, we may observe that the Stage 1 decision, if it begins a family, clearly governs Stage 2 decisions: when to begin work and at what. Those who did not marry early retained more flexibility. At the close of Stage 2 (say, between twenty-five and thirty), those families who will be poor are readily recognized. Early marriage and child-bearing, incomplete education, a poor first job, a chaotic work history—any two of these qualities mean a family at high risk of being poor most of the time. Members of such a family are unlikely to change matters very much through their own efforts. A recent study in California, seeking to distinguish between people who receive public assistance and those who do not, confirms this conclusion. The author writes:

3 5

The main factor involved in the unemployment, underemployment and dependency of the welfare group is not deviant attitude, or deviant personality, but the high-risk objective circumstances of being relatively under-skilled, under-educated, and over-sized.

. . . These high-risk circumstances are shared by a substantial segment of the population which is not currently on welfare . . . but is likely to be at any given time in the future.[6, 25]

FAMILY CYCLE SQUEEZE—THE CONFLICT OF ASPIRATION AND NEED

In a study of men who carry more than one job—so-called moonlighters—Harold Wilensky found them to be not necessarily poor, or rich, or in between. Rather the moonlighter is, typically, a man of any income, squeezed between not unreasonable ambitions and family needs he could never quite satisfy. The key, which Wilensky calls "life cycle squeeze," is not the man's age but the stage of his family development and especially the number of his children. Wilensky writes:

. . . The American man most likely to moonlight would be a young, educated Negro with many children, a job such as ward attendant, and a chaotic work history. His mother, a sales clerk whose husband deserted years ago, has fired him with old-fashioned ambition; his wife, a part-time cleaning woman, wants to escape from the ghetto. He is a clerk in his spare time.[225]

In the end the moonlighter does not realize his ambitions. The needs of his family move more rapidly than he; he has neither surplus money nor energy. Typically he is blocked and feels deprived.

Thus Wilensky has established a dynamic relationship between aspiration and need for a special group, perhaps 6 per cent of workingmen. (Because family structure determines the changing aspect of need, we prefer to call this relationship family cycle squeeze.) Almost all poor families must feel the squeeze, and obviously most respond otherwise than by moonlighting. Some men, though they would also seek a second job, work too many hours at their first job.[225] As we shall see, some poor families send the mother to work, even when the children are relatively young.

Some families take the opposite course; instead of expanding their income, they adjust their needs to their income or even reduce them. For instance, they may space their children so that their needs can be absorbed. Those who are destined to be poor appear to have a second child three or four months closer to the first than do others.[36, 68] Another way some families limit their needs is to restrict the number of their children. That families do take these steps has been demonstrated over and over again, and various studies suggest that at least a number of such families manage to move up a step or two.* [111] The variety of ways of meeting needs illustrates what is anyway plausible. The more members there are in a family, the more income is needed. The necessity to devote all income and more to current needs is associated with the inability to make progress.

Beyond this point, discussion frequently mires down in an inability to demonstrate either, on the one hand, that people have children for the same reasons for which they are poor (a tendency to live in the present, etc.) or, on the other hand, that the facts of poverty make it difficult to control the number of births. We know

---

* For other citations of studies which relate status and fertility, see Ronald Freedman.[62] Certain studies produced inconclusive or negative results if their samples were small or special, if they did not discriminate between families that could afford children and families that could not, or if the hypothesis was formulated too grandly. For example, one study stated the "economic tension" hypothesis: "The greater the difference between the actual level of living and the standard of living desired, the higher the proportion of couples practising contraception effectively and the smaller the planned families." [155] With a hypothesis stated so extremely, the findings would be blurred both by large families quite unrealistic about their aspirations and small families quite realistic about their chances for improvement.

that poor people have not had the required attitudes, skills, or access to medical resources to practice effective birth control.[150] But these facts lend themselves to either of the above interpretations; in fact the two arguments are probably different political views of the same facts. For, seen day by day, the family that cannot control its course does not seek to control its course, and the reverse is also true. The point is, however, that the squeeze is felt every day. Whatever its origin, above some threshold the imbalance becomes a hindrance rather than a stimulus to self-improvement.

There is a sprinkling of evidence that the fourth or fifth child represents a point of no return for poor families. The California study cited above concluded that families with four or more children face a substantial risk of poverty.[25] A study of families during periods of unemployment concluded that families with four or more children "found it considerably more difficult to manage financially." The more drastic means of managing—"borrowing money, piling up bills, moving to cheaper quarters, and going on relief—all show sharp increases with size of family." [32] A third study notes that separations and desertions tend to occur at the time the wife is pregnant. "A major point of pressure for the low income male," observes the author, "appears to be an increase in family size with no comparable increase in family income or earning capacity." [108] An independent study of AFDC families "seemed to indicate that fathers return [to their families] when they are able to support them." [76] If four- or five-child families face a special problem, one would expect the children to reflect it. About seven out of every ten youths rejected by Selective Service come from families with four or more children.[145]

Table 3–2 sums up the risk of poverty in terms of family size. Adding a third or fourth child raises the incidence of poverty by 6 per cent, but the next children raise the incidence by 13 percentage points each. "For many families," writes the researcher

who developed these figures, "a critical point in financial status
may be the arrival of the fourth or fifth child." [138]

TABLE 3–2. *Per Cent of Families Who Were Poor in 1963*

NUMBER OF RELATED CHILDREN UNDER EIGHTEEN YEARS OF AGE	PER CENT OF FAMILIES WHO WERE POOR
None, one, or two	12
Three children	17
Four children	23
Five children	36
Six or more children	49

Source: Mollie Orshansky, "Counting the Poor: Another Look at the Poverty
Profile," *Social Security Bulletin*, Vol. 28, No. 1 (January 1965).[138]

Although these figures make the point about risk, they are
averages and inevitably crude. It is possible to get somewhat closer
to various family types by examining the occupations of the men
whose wives have had the most children. These figures (still averages, to be sure) hint at a more common-sense, though complex,
relation of birth rate and income. The white men who have the
most children work, in descending proportions, as farm laborers
and foremen, miners, plasterers, carpenters, truck drivers, and
physicians. These are the lowest- and highest-paid occupations
listed by the census for those for whom number of children can be
determined. Their incomes fell, more or less, below $5,000 or, for
physicians, above $19,000. (The pattern for Negro families does
not include any high-fertility, high-income occupational groups.
This is consistent with the previous observation that disadvantaged
families moving up are more likely to restrict the size of their
family severely.) By contrast, families averaging about three children or fewer per mother are bunched in the occupational range
between $4,000 and $9,000, with a scattering up to $15,000.[200, 202]

39

Thus several children are not necessarily a bar to decent income, but income is either high enough to support several children or very low indeed; for families of four or five children or more there is no in-between. Other evidence supports this point. The more children there are in an AFDC family, the more the mother owes.[76] The more children there are in a poor family, the larger is the proportion of needed income that the family lacks.[138]

Children are the most significant element in the family cycle squeeze, but they are not the only element. Large families face many types of special difficulty. In finding housing they experience great hardship; even public housing, for example, is less likely to prove a resource. A mother with five children cannot as readily go to work as a mother with two. Yet the problem of a large family is only a midstream example of imbalance between needs and resources. The eighteen-year-old couple with one child faces an imbalance in the same sense. The problem of the mother without a husband may also be read as a type of family cycle squeeze. She has very nearly the same financial needs but much less in the way of resources than a mother with a husband. (In the past decade the median income of such families increased only about half as fast as that of all families.) [8] Entirely apart from children, the relatives of those who are poor are also likely to be poor. As mothers and fathers approach forty, *their* parents enter their sixties and may have serious need of financial or other kinds of care.[166] One study of families receiving public assistance shows that the majority of recipients with relatives were giving rather than receiving help.[100]

For all these reasons, need may manage to exceed resources by too wide a margin, forcing choices that are likely to defeat the family. The sorts of choices that are forced have already been noted: limited education, limited mobility, dead-end jobs, and family breakdown. Moreover, the couple in their thirties have children growing into adolescence. The quality of their nurture, education, and family life has been affected right along. By adolescence they begin to make the same categorical choices—more school or less, whether to begin a family early or not. The strains implicit in the life cycle of any family have been recognized for some time. But poor families, whose need is likely continually to outpace resources, are disadvantaged in a tight descending spiral; and in the end statistics reflect the spiral. The same people have many children, poor education, unemployment, broken families, and so forth. What else is new!

We are in a position, with the material in Stage 2, to illustrate the type of program question that may be raised. On the whole, families tend to start receiving public assistance late in the game. This is not because they don't apply early enough. It is because essentially the same families, with fewer children, are initially rejected for AFDC as are granted assistance later, when they have more children.[183, 20] If accepted for assistance, smaller families receive it for a shorter period of time.[20] With stipulated exceptions in a number of states, acquiring a larger income than minimum requirements becomes the occasion for discontinuing assistance. Standards for minimum requirements are themselves low; in 1963 the standards were approximately as high as our definition of poverty in only six states. In the majority of states, assistance will not be provided if a husband or other man is at home. In short, while the program may relieve desperate need, it deliberately avoids creating any surplus that might provide room for maneuvering. Thus AFDC is a recognizable element of the poor family's world, alleviating need but not providing the flexibility that might tend to alter the direction in which the family is moving. These policies reflect the necessity to distribute insufficient resources equitably, as well as the necessity to be seen to discourage malingering. But from the point of view of objectives, such policies exhibit a curious ambivalence. In a wide variety of ways over the past few years, the program has bent toward helping to prevent dependency; yet AFDC tends to operate too parsimoniously and too late to turn the tide of family cycle squeeze.

41

FAMILY BREAKDOWN

In view of everything we have discussed, it can come as no surprise that many poor families in time become unable to maintain an intact family or a steady income. Some will have reached this stage by the age of twenty, having already achieved two or three children and a chaotic family and work history. Others will have struggled doggedly, perhaps experiencing moments of hope but yielding in the end. We have seen some of the elements in this outcome; they require now to be brought together.

We noted that those who married early would tend to break up; only half the women who married at seventeen or earlier would still be living with the same husband thirty years later. We also noted that half the women who married at seventeen have (about) four children or more. Finally we observed that large families create unbearable pressure on men with low incomes. These facts are not independent; taken together they suggest that mothers in broken families are likely to have more children than those in stable families. Odd as this may seem, it is indeed a fact. "Among those females who were mothers by 1960, wives had an average of 2.9 children ever born, and female heads [of families] had an average of 3.7 children ever born. (That the two groups were somewhat different in age and color accounted for only a third of the difference.)" [8]

The pattern that these medians and percentages represent is not difficult to discern. The early, low-income marriage may begin poorly or it may begin well and earnestly. The problem is not necessarily in the manner of beginning but rather in providing the "means for the young adult to meet the demands of marriage and not become a marriage dropout." [108] However, with inadequate education and training, money becomes a grave problem. With a second or third child, the marriage may well show strain. When a

42

middle-class marriage shows strain, the wife may settle for being supported comfortably, even if she is unhappy. The wife whose husband is poor cannot make such a compromise.[108] It has been observed that even unmarried mothers will reject marriage if the prospective husband is viewed as an economic liability.* [15, 163] From the wife's point of view, as well as from the husband's, strain may readily lead to separation or divorce.

Following separation, there may be reconciliation or the wife may make an arrangement with another man. Both divorce and separation are common among poor families, despite the common impression that separation replaces divorce.[28] In general, two thirds of divorced women remarry,[70] and young women are even more likely to remarry. That is, whether a family is broken by separation or divorce, the chances are high that a new family will be formed. In that case the pressures continue and, with a very small likelihood of there being reasonable support payments for the children, the new family is more heavily burdened. Some of these second attempts work out, but more do not.[9] The path that opens before a family is a sequence of marriages or liaisons in which the notion of a stable intact marriage, if it was ever present, becomes fainter. One study of economically dependent families observes:

> Many of the women who were currently divorced, separated or deserted had been in such situations previously and expected to have similar experiences in future. . . . This repetition in behavior was hard for the women we interviewed to explain.[96]

How, indeed, *explain* a response to circumstances that seems natural and even inevitable? The sound of this pattern is grim. The saving grace, perhaps, for people who reflect such a pattern is that they are sufficiently numerous and walled off by neighbor-

---

* No researcher in the latter-day sense, G. B. Shaw had a character say in *Heartbreak House:* "If I can't have love, there's no reason why I should have poverty."

hoods and modes of communication that many regard it as a common, fated way of life.* [83, 124]

We set out to uncover the family-income cycle with couples who married young; although the overall chances are smaller, some who marry later follow the same course. It must be clear that progressive breakdown in family relations may be accompanied by breakdown in ability to secure a stable income. Without a husband, mothers are of course at a disadvantage. They may work, but their earnings are relatively low and they incur special costs. The process of divorce or separation itself involves costs (legal, dislocation) that are large for poor families.† If the man feels he must move, he may make a damaging job change. Confused legal relationships or casual work patterns may interfere with eligibility for survivors' insurance, unemployment compensation, and so forth. As we have noted, children may be withdrawn from school, making for later difficulty. All these costs would be significant for any family; for poor families, they add to an already intolerable squeeze.

As the main focus of our attention is income, we have no more than hinted at the extensive research that has been done concerning the feelings associated with deprivation.‡ Such material would substantiate the critical nature of each of the stages so far discussed but might distract us from the simple relationships of money and family development. However, in order to underline the fact that feeling must accompany deprivation, we offer the following excerpt from a researcher's interview. A woman sup-

---

* Said one man: "Here people are equals. They're all scuffling just like me." [49]

† An indirect confirmation of this point is offered by women describing "the two most important elements in surviving on assistance: staying on good terms with your landlord so that you do not have to move often and not running up a food bill if you can help it." [100]

‡ See *The Eighth Generation*,[159] *Blue Collar Marriage*,[99] *And the Poor Get Children*,[150] *The Culturally Deprived Child*,[157] *The Children of Sanchez*,[109] and articles by Hylan Lewis[108] and Walter Miller.[124]

porting four children on $27.50 a week, in the stage we describe as family breakdown, explains:

> If a man has anything and offers to help you out, you don't say to him: "But you'll have to marry me first," she said. You take what he offers right off and offer what you have in return. Of course, you hope that someday he will want to make it legal. But beggars can't be choosers.
>
> I don't drink whiskey but once in a while I'll get myself a half pint of gin. . . . But that's about all I spend on myself. I ain't had a new dress for about three years. . . . I don't go nowhere to need a new dress.
>
> If there's one thing I want it's a back yard, fenced in, so my children don't have to play out in the street. . . . I sure hope and pray that someday I can do better. But what can I do now? [110]

By definition, parents who reach their forties poor have not managed to achieve a decent income. A substantial percentage are no longer married and some of the rest have troubled marriages. The two problems are interconnected. The income problem is a source of reinfection for each new marriage, and each marital failure is likely to add to the income problem.

STAGE 5

We originally proposed only four stages of family-income development; Stage 5 is actually Stage 1 for the next generation. During each of the stages children have been growing older. As parents experience Stages 3 and 4, their children are entering Stages 1 and 2. Even if their parents have managed to avoid separation or divorce and certainly if they have moved into Stage 4, the children tend to begin their families early and make poor career choices. They make the same mistakes as their parents for the same reasons: little help and example, not enough money to support longer-term alternatives, little hope of doing better, little practical access to ways of doing better. We mentioned that the rules of the game may be felt more powerfully at the end of Stage 1. The rule for these children, growing through their parents' third and fourth stages, reads: Go back to Stage 1 and retrace the moves your parents made.

CONCLUSION

It is a platitude of occupational research that the father's occupation determines the son's. As we discern the complex and powerful forces that shape choices related to income, we are able to make a more exact statement: The father's family and financial circumstances determine the son's, and the circumstances that surround them both determine occupational choice.

We have attempted to distinguish four critical stages in the family and income development of poor people. These may assist us in visualizing poor families in the stream of life rather than as fractions of a population or at a given point in time. The method of visualizing flow used here is easily as imperfect as an early kinescope—we project a series of snatches of life and trust to imagination to provide the intervals. Research that will provide a sharper, truer image is badly needed.

The method of describing stages as we have used it concentrates on the common set of circumstances at each stage rather than the variety of families moving through the stage. It is important at least to bear in mind, however, that the same pressures are experienced by various kinds of families who respond in different ways. They differ in color, in urbanity, in geography, and in devotion to one another. They differ in native endowment, in attachment to neighborhood or social groups, and in sheer luck. Very likely a number of types of families are distinguishable according to these and other criteria, but we do not know how many types or which move through these stages to their grim conclusion because research into poverty has not yet sought to distinguish them.

Apart from the detail offered in this chapter, these general conclusions may be drawn:

1. Money, as it is paid out by an employer or government agency, may be regarded as going to individuals. Spending can only be understood, however, as pooled family spending for family needs.

2. A policy that is functional in terms of moving people out of poverty provides them with surplus money and time—provides them with capital. The situation of families taking off from poverty is analogous to that of developing countries. Take-off awaits "the build-up of social overhead capital," together with the necessary skills and a drive for improvement.[160] Take-off for poor families requires surplus money for investment in self-improvement, as well as the skill and drive more usually asked of them. To support people at minimal income may represent responsible and even charitable public policy. If it does not pass the threshold of minimum subsistence and provide some surplus, however, it is not a functional anti-poverty program.

3. The stages of family-income development suggest that leverage may more readily be provided at some points than at others. As we have seen, each stage prejudices the next. Therefore, the two stages most open to influence from outside are, in rather different senses, the earliest. The first is the period when a couple is just starting out, for they may at that time be induced to postpone having children and to make wiser (and usually more expensive) choices about training and work. The second occurs after the first children have reached adolescence, at which time they may be influenced to postpone beginning a family of their own, at least until a girl is eighteen or nineteen and a boy somewhat older.

4 7

What is involved here is not regulating or advising against marriage but making possible a total pattern in which early marriage does not become attractive or obligatory. It should be unnecessary to say this except that, as Marianne Moore has written, "the passion for setting people right is itself an afflictive disease."

4. It is not just the availability of money at any given moment that influences the course poor families take but their expectation that money will be available for certain purposes. Therefore, a *functional* program, in terms of setting them on a course leading out of poverty, will be predictable and, where necessary, continuous. Families will not only receive money but understand the comparatively simple conditions that determine whether they receive it. And income will not be subject to discontinuance because new policies are devised from year to year or because the funds of a demonstration program run out.

In short, an income maintenance program may rightly be viewed as an expression of social justice; it may also be viewed as an investment in the careers of our citizens. When it is so viewed, we are required to ask what are the crucial periods in which the investment may have an effect, in the grip of what forces children are held and how that grip may be relieved, not how little but how much is required to achieve such a *détente*, and what is the most businesslike fashion in which to proceed. If we ask the questions, we begin to find answers.

4

Who Are Meant to Work?

✚✚✚✚✚✚✚✚✚✚✚✚✚✚✚✚✚✚✚✚

A national program that sustains income must be designed in relation to income from work—especially its effect upon the incentive to work. To understand this relationship we must shift from a broad view of environmental forces to a narrower view of a particular program's impact on a man's conception of his self-interest. We have also to ask for whom it is socially desirable to provide the maximum incentive to work. First, however, we should note that persuasive arguments can be made for treating the incentive to work as inconsequential.

It has been argued with some force that the role of work as the primary source of income is changing. The capacities of cybernetic equipment are so great that we can no longer expect the need for new workers to expand rapidly enough to compensate for increased productivity. It is said on the contrary that wages will no longer offer a reasonable method of distributing the nation's income. Robert Theobald, who first assembled this argument, proposes that means other than wages and salaries be found to get money to people.[190]

Unfortunately no basic data are available for an explicit test of this argument—that cybernation is moving at a new rate and we face a revolution as drastic as that introduced by industrialization. Productivity appears to be increasing at the rate of about 3 per cent a year. From 1909 to 1947 productivity increased at the rate of about 2 per cent a year. These figures suggest a gain but no revolution. It may be argued that the full possibilities of cybernation are not reflected in productivity. Unions, management, and governmental units may resist or retard modernization for fear of unemployment and conflict with labor. If income were freed from wages, might cybernation move faster? It is impossible to say.

Moreover, the rate at which productivity is moving is not in itself decisive. For one thing, requirements that men work are being diminished, as indeed Theobold says they should be. We are paying more for a somewhat reduced work week. We are keeping youths in school longer and providing them with income in various ways. We are slowly bringing down the accepted age of retirement and liberalizing the benefits given to retired people. A new income maintenance program for children would, in still another form, provide income separate from work. At the same time it is the tritest of observations that automation may lead to new industry and new jobs. In the end it is not clear what the influence of automation has been. Robert Solow put the point as follows:

> It is possible that any particular burst of technological progress will carry along with it the extra demand necessary to keep extra unemployment from appearing. It is also possible that it will not . . . One can, of course, say whether unemployment has gone up or gone down. But there are many other influences on employment. Faster growth of the labor force, for example, can also push up the capacity trend; it can also have effects on demand. Except under the best of circumstances, it may prove impossible to identify the particular effects of technical progress and separate them from the effects of other forces.[177]

With the evidence pointing to only a modest improvement in productivity and that readily offset in other ways, it is not surprising that the National Commission on Technology, Automation and Economic Progress in 1966 concluded that automation was not in itself likely to lead to serious economic changes. A historian looking back from the year 2000 may judge that Theobald was right in his estimate of the possibilities of cybernation but that the sharp break with precedent which he called for had been subverted by conservatism, compromise, and conspicuous consumption. However it may seem in retrospect, we assume that work will be the major source of family income for at least several decades to come.

Even if one accepts that our society will continue to need work, a more modest argument may be made for ignoring incentive in the case of one segment of the population—those who have the poorest incomes. It has variously been proposed that we are now wealthy enough to assure all families a minimum income of $3,000 or $1,500.[190, 79] Those who fail to earn the specified amount would have the difference made up by the government. Thus below the established floor, in effect, a dollar earned would mean a dollar lost in government benefits. Numbers are not im-

51

portant here; in principle all such proposals ignore the question of incentive below a specified level. The argument is likely to be conducted instead in terms of minimum wages and social justice.

For example, will a man who can expect to work regularly at the legally established minimum (say, $1.40 an hour) reject even such an offer for an assured income of $1,500? From the point of view of a taxpayer, the same question is stated conversely: Can one really blame a man for being reluctant to work regularly for 75 cents an hour (the equivalent of $1,500 a year)? The issue raised by these questions is not whether incentive can or should be maintained, but whether it ought to be maintained by such socially unjust means as forcing people to work for miserable wages. It is whether people who are able to earn so little can be assumed thereby to be handicapped and so entitled to support even at the expense of incentive.

It cannot be said that the nation has an economic need to spur people in these circumstances to work. The total income deficit of all poor Americans has been valued at $11 or $12 billion.[48, 128, 138] If by ignoring incentive in their case we were to sacrifice even twice that value in production, we should have lost less than one year's increment in production. Yet obviously the question of incentive to work calls forth a deeper response from Americans than an assessment of the economic need for work. The tendency to despise those thought to be getting something for nothing runs very deep in Americans. More attempts have been made to wipe out the Elizabethan Poor Law than were made on Elizabeth's life; yet the contemptuous attitudes associated with it survive. It is these attitudes, deeply rooted and apparently unchanging, that force us to make an issue of the incentive to work. Besides, those beneficiaries who think they are receiving a free ride may themselves feel uneasy or unworthy.

That we attend to incentive as a result of our own values rather than out of sheer economic need has implications for us. First, the values are presumably subject to change; at least that is the hope of those who make the modest argument for ignoring incentive. Second, the values conflict with others concerning the rights of children and social responsibility for those who are unfortunate. We must be prepared for difficulty in finding public policy which can support diverse and even antagonistic objectives.

We will discuss in the following pages the relationship of income maintenance programs to patterns of work. First, is the incentive to work influenced in general by income maintenance? Second, what effect do we *wish* to have on the work patterns of women? Do we wish to encourage them to work, to discourage them, or to encourage some but not others?

We do not seek a rule to bind people; this would be contrary to our convictions about the rights of families to make their own choices. But an income maintenance program and its policies (or their absence) make some choices practical and others unavailable. We may not convincingly disguise what we encourage or discourage by saying that we never meant to influence people at all. Moreover, the decisions we abdicate as a matter of policy will be made operationally, conceivably with an admixture of personal attitude or prejudice.*

INCENTIVE TO WORK— MEN AND WOMEN

It is well that we treat the issue of incentive to work after reviewing the family-income cycle. We are aware at the outset that atti-

---

* For example, when studied several years ago, the percentage of AFDC mothers who worked varied between whites and Negroes and among states. Across the nation 10 per cent of white mothers worked and 23 per cent of nonwhite mothers. In Mississippi, the state with the highest percentage, 24 per cent of white mothers worked and 63 per cent of nonwhite mothers.[209] One must suspect on the basis of these figures that decisions not made in federal law or administration were being made in state capitals and county seats. For discussions of the tendencies of bureaucracies in dealing with unsettled policy issues, see *The Dynamics of Bureaucracy*[12] and *Decisions about People in Need*.[95]

tudes toward work and career may be shaped while a child is in diapers, by events that seem remote from the work he will do later. In this sense, those resources and patterns that contribute to sound development in a child also contribute to his later incentive to work and to his ability to develop a progressive and remunerative career. The issue is usually viewed in a short-term sense, however, as the direct response of an adult to a choice between income maintenance and earnings.

The assumption that income maintenance payments influence work has a long and, from a current point of view, not entirely honorable history. Shortly before the American revolution Arthur Young could observe tranquilly that "everyone but an idiot knows that the lower classes must be kept poor, or they will never be industrious." [236] Rather more recently Senator Douglas, advancing a proposal for family allowances, found it necessary to counter the argument that they "would lessen the energy with which men worked and hence would decrease output." [43] The expansion of income maintenance programs has, on the contrary, been accompanied by increased economic growth and increased productivity. Our appetite for income has advanced very satisfactorily ahead of our ability to satisfy it; reputable economists no longer argue that the threat of poverty is needed to induce "work and sobriety." [102, 33] To transmute this economic observation into a psychological one, it is no longer respectably argued that the provision of, say, a thousand dollars a year (from the government? from dividends?) keeps a man from striving for several thousand.

The issue that continues to be treated seriously concerns marginal incomes. What is the effect on particular families—who may be weary, or poorly motivated, or have a long history of deprivation—if they are provided with a minimum income? With the question focused on particular families that may subside into inertia, every man has his own anecdote to tell but virtually no quantitative assessment is possible. Relevant data are available only if one phrases the question somewhat differently: What will families do if program income is reduced when there is income from work? Conversely, how will families behave if the combined income from a program and from work is permitted to be significantly more than from a program alone? The evidence indicates that people will work if it brings them profit and will not work if it does not.

One can demonstrate in Aid to Families with Dependent Children an "apparent tendency" for women to work where they gain monetary advantage and to stay at home where they do not.[168] (Evidently Congress was convinced of this point; in 1965 it provided that specified amounts of income could be permitted without affecting AFDC assistance payments.) A similar problem has dogged public housing, where increased earnings may lead to higher rents, if not to eviction. Old people on social security offer evidence relevant to the question of whether the incentive to work is affected by the relation of income and earnings. Social security payments appear to encourage retirement and part-time work.[74, 67] The argument that their income will barely change leads some men to *early* retirement.[58] At the same time, men receiving social security benefits chafe under a too rigid earnings limitation. Therefore, in the past few years the earnings limit has been altered to allow beneficiaries to retain at least some portion of a greater amount of earnings.

In short, people with marginal income will work, despite program income, if they gain from work. At the margin at which there is no financial gain in work, many will decide against it. The point seems simple and plausible enough. Why should anyone doubt it? Confusion arises from two directions. On one hand, the concept is broadened to imply that *any* payment without work or any tax upon earnings will sap the willingness to work. As we have said, it is impossible any longer to sustain this point of view. On the other hand, the observation that people will not work without personal benefit is taken as an attack on the will to self-dependence. There can be no doubt that some people, very poor or very wealthy, work simply out of pride or pleasure. But the primary goal people give in working, when they are asked, is money. It is no insult to imply that monetary advantage influences the decision to work and how to work. It goes without saying that other factors also affect people—their age, whether they are men or women, with children or without, well or ill, or able to command interesting work and status. Many will work despite small returns; some will fail to work who might benefit much.

The fact that people respond to self-interest must lead to at least two types of policy decision. First, the attempt may be made to develop a program that is largely neutral in relation to the incentive to work. Survivors' insurance very nearly achieves this. A mother may have adequate benefits if she remains at home. She may lose only the benefit payable to herself, not benefits payable to her children, if she decides to work. The pension that a veteran receives for a service-connected disability is neutral with respect to work. He receives the payment whether or not he works. He is assured of some degree of maintenance; to the extent that he can earn, he improves his income. Neutral programs may, to be sure, influence the total number of people who work by making it possible for some not to work. The concept of neutrality is meant here as an expression of whether or not *individuals* feel able to make a free choice. Those people do not feel able to make a free choice who are caught in a trap in which they are deterred from doing the very thing that might help them—that is, earning money when their income is low.

The blocking of free choice occurs when programs are keyed to earnings; the more drastically earnings affect payments, the more difficulties result. Such programs require a second type of policy decision. It becomes necessary to examine who are to be encouraged to work and who not to work: to examine the precise points at which deterrence operates and to devise mechanisms to cope with the effects. Eveline Burns has listed measures that have been taken to cope with the incentive problem:[21]

1. Make the receipt of benefits so unpleasant that people will work if they can. Publication of the names of beneficiaries has been used for this purpose.

2. Apply a test of need, thus combining deterrence with administrative assurance that the family's circumstances justify assistance.

3. Restrict the program to beneficiaries with income over a certain level. With low income earners excluded, reasonably high benefits can be paid without approaching too closely to wage levels of potential beneficiaries.

4. Base benefits upon some test of attachment to the labor force, thus assuring that the beneficiary normally works.

5. Limit the duration of benefits, so that program cost is self-limiting and the beneficiary knows he must eventually work.

All these measures have been tried at one time or another. They may be especially unsuitable for meeting the problem of childhood poverty. The first two measures, if they are felt as a penalty, operate upon children who cannot themselves be held responsible. The last three measures would tend to omit from coverage the very children who concern us.

It is also possible to devise a scale of benefits that varies with income, giving the beneficiary some portion of his earnings up to a point where it is advantageous for him to do without benefits entirely. Thus non-service-connected pensions for veterans vary inversely with income. As the scale works out, increasing his earnings or other personal income invariably proves advantageous to the veteran. Finally, administrative provisions may be built into a program to assure that men will work when they can. They may receive benefits, for example, only if they can show that they did not leave work voluntarily; or they may be required to accept rehabilitation or employment services.

To sum up, no program reasonably likely to be enacted would have extreme results upon incentive. No program would reduce the vigor with which workers work or would lead millions of people to prefer not to work at all. A program that relates payments inversely to current earnings may create two limited problems: (1) people whose incomes cannot exceed benefit levels, no matter what they do, may doubt whether it will ever pay to earn their own income; (2) if benefits decline when there are earnings, people at any income level (except, perhaps, the highest) may experience a sense of undue restriction. This sense of restriction may operate to keep poor families poor. Therefore, programs that relate payments to income require painstakingly designed policies and benefit formulas.

Several qualifications of this treatment of incentive should be borne in mind. An income maintenance program, even if it presents an incentive problem for adults, may contribute to sound development and incentive in their children. Second, the discussion has been limited to work *for pay*. Quite a number of people work without receiving money payment at all, most particularly women in the home. The point has been made by the two B's of social security—Beveridge and Burns—in order to argue that unpaid housework should provide as much of a basis as paid work for inclusion in income maintenance programs.[11] We shall return to this point. Finally, how can we fail to note our solemn assumption that people with a large income strive for more, whereas people with rather little are required to prove that they will do the same?

SHOULD WOMEN WORK?

Before World War II the desirable impact of public policy upon the employment of women was easy to state. In the mood of the depression and after, many felt that a woman who worked took a job away from a man. Studies confirmed the widespread conviction that if mothers worked their children suffered. Nor were women eager to work. The jobs that were open to them—clerical, sales, domestic, certain types of factory work—were not calculated to lure them from keeping house. It could be assumed that, with a few exceptions, those women who worked did so out of financial need. In 1940, for example, fewer than a third of the women who worked were living with husbands,[197] and those were women "from low-income families [who] worked as a matter of economic necessity." [165] Public policy, the consensus went, should support the perceptible wish of women to remain at home.

The war required a marked increase in the employment of women, in circumstances in which they patently supported rather than undermined the men of the country. Later, high unemployment and anxiety about cybernation might have produced a return to the feeling that women should stay at home, but much had changed between 1940 and 1960. First, more attractive work was opening up to women. They were entering the professions and white-collar employment more, factories and domestic service less. The change was particularly marked for Negro women. Twenty years ago 60 per cent of working Negro women were domestics, compared with 36 per cent today.[215] Many would-be employers of domestic help have felt the effects of this shift, whether or not they have understood it.

Second, woman's income is no longer viewed in terms of sheer necessity. Despite a steady general increase in income, by 1960 well over half of working women were married and living with their husbands.[197] The sharpest increase in percentage for wives who work has occurred among those whose husbands have the highest incomes.[165] Most women say, as they did two decades ago, that they work mainly to earn money, but obviously not all are now buying basic necessities.[133, 36]

A final change since 1940 is a considerable reinterpretation of the emotional effects of women going to work. It was widely assumed that when mothers worked their children were made vulnerable to delinquency or less visible difficulties—anxiety, slowed learning. Prewar research that supported this assumption has since been criticized as poorly controlled. A World Health Organization study, which also supported this assumption, was addressed to the consequences of the total separation of a child from his mother.[16] After several years it began to be pointed out that "maternal deprivation," when total, was different from the separation experienced when a mother worked.

Recent research finds only small differences in behavior and adjustment between children of working and nonworking mothers. When a mother works, whether or not she makes systematic arrangements for child care does appear to affect the child. If she does not, the child may be damaged.[181] Some say that the pendulum has swung too far toward the view that maternal work is benign. The effects on children are complex—related, for example, to how a woman feels about working—and may be ferreted out with sophisticated methods.[81] At any rate, debate about the consequences for children when mothers work now ranges on a fairly short tether around a post labeled "not proved."

Curiously the bulk of research has been concerned with school-age children (and white children at that). However, the maternal deprivation thesis has special force in connection with preschool children. Consequently scattered findings that preschool children are untouched by their mothers' going to work are being met with some doubt.[5] The general pattern of mothers' employment lends support to this doubt. The chances that a mother will work are three times as high if all her children are of school age. Poor women (whose husbands earn less than $3,000) with school-age children are more than *twice* as likely to work as those whose husbands earn more than $10,000. But poor women with preschool children are nearly *four* times as likely to work as those whose husbands earn more than $10,000.[165] Two forces seem to be operating here. Women tend not to work when they have preschool children, whatever their income level. Of those with preschool children who do work, many must be responding to stark need. Why do women with young children refrain from working? Certainly they have greater difficulty arranging for the care of children and household if the children are young. There is evidence too that the role of mother is more satisfying when children are young.* [133] These two factors—the systematic arrangements for child care and the way mothers feel about working—seem to combine to determine whether children are damaged when their mothers work.

Children are not the only ones who experience emotional effects when women go to work. Shifts also take place in the woman's view of herself and in her relationship with her husband. The wife tends to gain a greater voice in major economic decisions, while the husband gains a voice in routine household decisions. He also takes on more domestic tasks. In an "appreciable" number of families these changes create marital conflict.[13] Finally, work gives to many women a feeling of independence, equality, or achievement. It is difficult to say whether the net effect of work for women is positive, but certainly the public evaluation has shifted. The net effect once tended to be viewed as entirely destructive. It is now seen as complicated and perhaps dependent on the family situation.

To sum up so far, people are being encouraged to withdraw from the labor market in various ways—through schooling, retirement, and a shorter work week. With substantial unemployment it must be supposed that this trend would continue; it would be surprising if it did not again raise the question of employment for women.† On the other hand, employment for women is now a matter of self-realization. It has been absorbed (along with install-

* Says a character in *Heartbreak House:* "The natural term of affection of the human animal for its offspring is six years."
† Those who are impressed with the accelerated tendency of women to work may think it unlikely that this right or tendency will ever be questioned again. However, doubts about the trend persist. A 1961 survey of community opinions about day care found opposition to work for women a prominent reason for opposing the development of day care.[116]

ment credit) into the American family's concept of its potential income. The Department of Labor confidently predicts that employment of women will continue to expand. As for the effects of women's working on husband and children, social scientists have conveniently redefined the matter. The effects on the marital relationship are ambiguous. The effects on children are uncertain and may depend on the conditions associated with work rather than the fact of work. Serious doubt remains only as to the effects on preschool children of their mothers' working.

We may be ready now to advance an initial conclusion: Income maintenance programs for children should be directed toward making it possible for mothers with preschool children to stay at home. To put the matter cautiously, the weight of evidence leaves open the possibility that a preschool child may be damaged if his mother must work. In the evident resistance of mothers to working before their children attend school, one may see confirmation of this point. Alternatively that resistance may simply reflect how much harder it is to arrange a household when children are young, a point to which public policy should also be responsive. In coming to this conclusion we seek to be candid about the desired direction of an income maintenance program but not to undermine the observation that mothers should, in the end, make their own choices. How can these two views be combined?

The implied program would make available adequate money while the mother is at home. She would not be sought out as a likely prospect for employment and training. If our observations are accurate, many would decide not to work. The type of day care center that has been developed for working mothers (for preschool children all day, with pickup arrangements, and so on) would not, therefore, be required in quantity. However, the program might provide or at least not interfere with opportunities for the mother to maintain her skills so that she might return to work later. If she decided to work, she might lose a portion but not all of her benefits. Thus adequate benefits to a woman at home would encourage her to stay at home; however, work would be open to her without penalty.

It is more difficult to take an unequivocal position about mothers with older children. We are not prepared to say that all mothers with school-age children should be encouraged to stay at home. In recent public actions we have encouraged them to work. Without entering into the implications of varying state public assistance programs, we may say that recent federal legislation appears to lean toward increasing the number of working mothers. Extension of social services, work experience programs, and special income exemptions all encourage, if they do not actually press, mothers to work. Moreover, we do not expect school-age children, generally speaking, to be damaged because their mothers are at work.

Yet we are not prepared to say that *all* mothers with older children should work. Depending on their mothers' attitudes and circumstances, some school-age children may indeed be hurt. Those mothers who have special difficulty in working (disabled, poorly located), those who have large families, and those whose children have special needs have a special claim. Therefore, we envision that many mothers with older children will work but that a minority will choose not to work. This statement carries different policy implications from that concerning mothers with pre-school children. First, an income maintenance program may incorporate policies that encourage mothers to work. There may be training programs. There may be a requirement to make a showing that they should not work. Payment levels may decline when children have passed their sixth birthday. Second, if choices need to be made in programming or in funding, the younger children have priority.

Finally, we should make explicit a point that has been implied. Age classifications are a convention used to describe program policies. There are no women who are for all time mothers with preschool children. There are only young women who in time have children; while the mothers grow older, the children grow up and eventually leave home. It is important to visualize families over time for the following reasons. The mother with preschool children, if she remains at home, nevertheless needs to maintain or gain the skills that lead to work later on. As for the mother with older children who is unprepared for work, it is not permissible to deal with her as a generalization. Either she must be provided for or, if she is to work, she may need a new frame of reference and very special help.

5

Income and the
Birth Rate

✠✠✠✠✠✠✠✠✠✠✠✠✠✠✠✠✠✠✠

Population growth is a recurring issue in the United States. In the 1930's there was widespread anxiety that the population was not replacing itself. In the 1960's we are anxious because the population, not content with replacing itself, increases rapidly—with consequent crowding, dislocation, and pressure on services. In and out of public discussion weaves a strain of concern specifically with the birth rate of poor people. With a generally declining birth rate, it seemed that the poor might have most of the children; population quality—whether regarded as genetic or not—might decline. With a general rise in the birth rate, we are concerned that families already poor are handicapped by too many children and so are kept poor.

If we are to have public consideration of a major income maintenance program for children, questions will naturally be asked about the birth rate. Will total births rise? Will those who are poor be especially encouraged to have more children? Neither consequence is desirable. In Chapter 3 we discussed these questions in terms of individual family patterns. Now we must view them in terms of the probable effect on large population groups. We shall approach the available evidence in two ways: through the experience of other countries with rising income and family allowances, then by examining what factors affect fertility patterns in general.

NATIONAL EXPERIENCES

Viewed most broadly, the question about the impact of income support programs on the birth rate is a branch of a historic argument about economic growth and the birth rate. The view of classical economists was put by Adam Smith in these terms:

> If this demand [for labor] is continually increasing, the reward of labor must necessarily encourage in such a manner the marriage and multiplication of laborers, as may enable them to supply that continually increasing demand by a continually increasing population.[175]

As David McClelland points out, the argument that economic growth would lead to population growth was put forward at a time when England's population happened to be increasing. The number representing birth rate minus death rate in England was 0.7 or 0.8 in the period from 1750 to 1800 and rose to 1.2 in the period 1800 to 1950.[117] Population increase and economic growth were moving forward side by side. As so often happens, observers saw a law in the correlation.

If one abandoned the perspective of the early nineteenth century, however, and looked backward from 1940, quite the opposite trend was apparent. "The large declines in fertility in economically developed countries in the nineteenth and twentieth centuries are probably unprecedented." [62] Now a plausible correlation seemed to reflect a reverse law of human behavior: rising wealth is associated with a *declining* birth rate. Many explanations were advanced for this law. Their core was more sociological in tone: family functions, structure, and expectations change in an advancing industrial society. The new law gained an appearance of breadth by encompassing two observations of rather a different quality. Inside the developed countries, those people with higher incomes have lower birth rates. The underdeveloped nations, where wealth is slight, have higher birth rates.

There matters rested until after World War II, when rates of fertility in the developed countries suddenly moved upward again. It was impossible for the sophisticated to return to the simple view represented in the quotation from Adam Smith above. Speculation about the reversal ranges from the hypothesis that the new birth rate reflects an unconscious reaction against the threat of atomic testing to human survival, all the way to the notion that after attaining a certain level of adequacy, people in effect buy another child with additional income. It is not necessary to explore the merits of various theories but only to note that broad national trends support no sweeping generalization. Economic growth in an industrial country may be coupled with a rising or a declining birth rate. There is no indication here of the likely effect of an income maintenance program on birth rates.

Economic growth is so broad a concept that it may mask

relationships that do exist. If we turn to national experience with income maintenance, a clearer relationship may emerge. As a number of countries established family allowances *in order to* increase the population, it seems reasonable to explore this type of program.

In neighboring Canada, which has a delicate mixture of Protestant and French Catholic citizens, the population issue received due attention before a program of family allowances was enacted. Then for more than a decade after, Canadian officials made recurrent attempts to evaluate the influence of the allowances on the birth rate. Joseph Willard, director of research of the Department of National Health and Welfare, reported in 1957:

> There is little or no evidence to support the contention that the Canadian legislation has resulted in a birth rate higher than otherwise would have been the case. If there is any demographic influence it may be through a favorable effect on the survival rate rather than through any impact the program may have on the birth rate, but this would also be difficult to substantiate through statistical evidence.[229]

Although official attention to the issue apparently waned with the evaporation of Canadian criticism of family allowances, data in the last decade are also consistent with Joseph Willard's judgment.

The Canadian birth rate had started slowly upward when allowance payments began (1945) and then rose sharply. This was, of course, the immediate postwar period. Since 1957 the birth rate has started downward again. Close analysis of these figures would make it clear that any effect of allowances in the first decade cannot be disentangled from the effects of demobilization and postwar prosperity. Perhaps the most telling illustration of this point is the close correspondence between birth rates in Canada and in the United States. (See Figure 5–1.) U.S. and Canadian fertility patterns are not identical (Canadians marry later, for example); probably some differences between the two

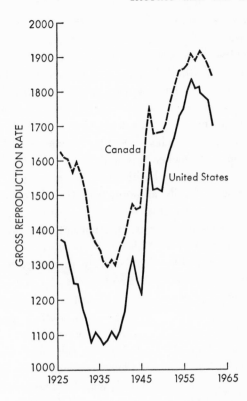

FIGURE 5–1. Gross reproduction rates, United States and Canada, 1926–62. Source: U. S. National Center for Health Statistics. Data on which the chart is based are shown in Appendix I.

countries cancel out. Nevertheless, it would be difficult to argue that the Canadian birth rate is responding to family allowances while the United States birth rate accompanies it up and down.

An exploration of fertility trends inside Canada yields statistics that may seem not only uninformative but perverse. If allow-

69

ances produce larger families, it might be argued that this would be seen most markedly where large families are most desired or most accepted. Thus one might have expected family growth to be most marked in Catholic Quebec. Yet the increase in births through 1956 was smaller in Quebec than in any other province. The fertility of married women at each specific age—a more complex but more accurate measure than total births—actually declined for every age group in Quebec except the youngest.[115] It is important now to note that Quebec was undergoing rapid urbanization in this period, as compared with the other provinces. Any population response to family allowances that might conceivably have appeared was overwhelmed by the response to urbanization.

The Canadian program was not intended to increase the birth rate; moreover, its cash payments are modest. That it produces no demonstrable effect on birth rates may tell us nothing about more ambitious programs of family allowances. Let us turn to the country that pays the most substantial benefits and deliberately sought a demographic result. As in other developed countries, the birth rate in France had moved steadily downward from 1800 to World War II. In 1945 the French social security system was reorganized and family allowances made virtually universal. In the five years before World War II, France had averaged 630,000 births a year. In the five years after the war (after the new family allowance program went into effect), the nation averaged 856,000 births a year. Total births declined slightly from this peak to a low point in 1953 and have shown a modest rise since.[146] As the total population has also been rising, the birth rate per thousand of population has varied little since 1954.[144]

One may understand from the marked reversal in 1945 why some French officials take the position that family allowances have increased fertility. Moreover, they are impressed by the more marked recovery of fertility in France than among its neighbors. (Still other European countries, such as Portugal and Poland, have higher fertility rates than France.)[195] French administrators and demographers seek a more cautious position. They say, for example, that family allowances contributed to a general natalist spirit which is now a force in itself. They account in this way for the maintenance of stable fertility rates during the past decade despite a relative decline in the significance of family allowances. (Family benefits were permitted to fall behind while wages were rising rapidly.)[141] If we reflect that Canada, with a modest family allowance program, and the United States, with none, experienced concurrent dramatic increases in the birth rate, we must be skeptical about even the more cautious formulation.

As with Canada, the components of the general increase in the French birth rate are difficult to reconcile with a view that family allowances are the causal element. One would expect family allowances to influence chiefly rural and other very poor French families. There is, for example, a wry country saying: "Let's make a baby to buy a motor bike." * But the data indicate that it is the urban families and those with comfortable incomes —not the others—that are showing the substantial increases in size.[85] Because of the way French family allowances are calculated, the major advantage is felt by families with three or more children. Therefore, if births were a consequence of family allowances, the number of large families should be increasing. What actually happened to create the sharp rise in the birth rate during the decade after the war was that more families had one, two, or three children while the proportion of large families diminished.[85, 146, 144]

Our major difficulty in determining what lessons Canada and France teach is that they initiated their programs when fertility rates would naturally have risen anyway. We may extend our range by noting countries where the birth rate barely rose

---

* A more sophisticated statement of the same sort opens a satirical autobiography: "I was born of Allowances and a Holiday, of which the morning stretched out happily to the sound of 'I love you You love me' played on a sweet trumpet." [158]

7 1

or even declined. Italy experienced a decline through the 1940's despite all efforts. Sweden suffered a continuing decline in its birth rate through the 1950's when the rate in most Western countries was high.[69] As for Nazi Germany, its "whole vast apparatus . . . was used with a concentrated ferocity to raise the birth rate." [192] Not only were allowances paid; bachelors were taxed and men with large families were given preference in employment. Births rose from 14.7 per thousand population in 1933 to 19.7 in 1938 but never approached the figures achieved earlier in the century (29.5 in 1910–13). Even the modest increase has been attributed to improved economic conditions and the suppression of abortion, in combination with cash allowances.[97] We cannot say of these countries that allowances failed to influence births, any more than we can say of France and Canada that they succeeded. It seems clear that in Italy and Sweden, at least, the birth rates were destined to decline. Whether allowances prevented a sharper decline cannot be known.

At the 1964 meetings of the International Social Security Association, the Permanent Committee on Family Allowances entertained a suggestion that the effects of allowances on birth rates be studied. The committee declined to undertake such a study at that time, reasoning that sufficient data would not be available to support responsible conclusions. We perceive how difficult it is to interpret the data. On the basis of national experiences, we can only leave the question open—neither proved nor disproved.

Having proffered the obligatory judgment, perhaps we may press one step further to a plausible one. On one hand, it seems likely that some undetermined number of families, particularly some with scant or moderate incomes, would have an additional child *because* it would bring them a government payment. These families may want a motor bike or they may simply enjoy children. On the other hand, national experiences suggest that the effect of such families on the national birth rate or its major elements (family size, births in low-income families as compared

7 2

with middle-income families, etc.) would probably be undetectable. Compared with other factors that seem to govern population trends (the general level of living, infant survival, etc.), an income maintenance program, however large, is small.

FACTORS INFLUENCING FERTILITY

We have been concentrating on national experience with rising income, particularly if the income comes from a national program. Turning away from the experience of other countries with income maintenance, we now ask what factors of any sort appear to influence fertility in the United States one way or another. In viewing the question in this fashion, we will be able to deal directly with such special tendencies of low-income families as may be discerned.

Consistent with the experience in western Europe, the birth rate in the United States has moved steadily downward over the long term. It is said that this long-term decline is compounded of (1) a shift in population from rural to urban areas, where having a large number of children is not economically useful to a family; (2) the spread in an urban society of efficient contraceptive devices and knowledge; (3) the shift from large, geographically stable families to small, movable families; and (4) new views of the relationship of the individual to society and to God which have tended to depreciate the value of children.[62] The decline reached bottom, so far as we can now tell, when women born between 1906 and 1910 completed child-bearing. They averaged 2.3 children each—thus being responsible for the lowest level of fertility since the Republic was founded.[220]

Despite the long-term trend, in the short run the birth rate moves up and down in a manner distinctly related to economic prosperity or depression. Hope Eldridge has made this observation in the following terms:

> Within this [long term] process, fluctuations in the birth rate show a positive correlation with fluctuations in the economic situation. People, like crops, are more prolific in "good years" than in "bad years." In population where fertility is largely subject to voluntary control [as in the developed countries] the timing of births adjusts itself to changes in the economic outlook. If, as recent studies suggest, levels in completed fertility are influenced by the duration and intensity of these adjustments, then it follows that economic policy . . . is in effect population policy.[50]

The point seems plausible: when times are bad, families restrict the number of their children in order to avoid extra expense. When times are good, they may catch up and even have more children. (The long-term trend is nevertheless maintained.)

For some time researchers have been interested in the possibility that it is not prosperity in any absolute sense that influences families.[78] Rather, families are influenced by the feeling that they have more or less income than others like themselves; or by the feeling that their own prospects are looking up or deteriorating. Deborah Freedman has calculated the income that men may expect to have, based on their occupation, education, and age. Studied in relation to these predictions, men whose income exceeds the norm have more children than average. Men with low incomes in relation to others like themselves have fewer children. The number of children is directly related to *relative* income.[61] Even more pointedly it has been argued that the link between prosperity and a high birth rate is the young adult entering the job market. If he has had a small income but his prospects are good, he will have a rather large family. If he is accustomed to a substantial income but jobs are hard to find, he will have fewer children. Thus young adults who grew up in the depression and married and worked after World War II had a high birth rate.[46] Those who grew up in better circumstances after 1940 and faced the (for youths) highly competitive job market of the early 1960's may be expected to have fewer children.[47] Indeed they seem to be doing so.

This material gives us several hints about the effect of an income maintenance program on birth rates. Any substantial increment in family income will improve a family's situation, and there may therefore be an immediate reflection in a higher birth rate. On the other hand, birth rates may be influenced by the comparatively unchanging circumstances of other, similar people and by independent economic factors, such as the job market. In terms of economic factors alone, the tendency of the birth rate to respond to financial improvement would be muffled. Whatever the immediate response of the birth rate, after several years the contribution of an income maintenance program would be incorporated into families' standard of living and lose its influence on their birth rate.

These hints, such as they are, greatly oversimplify the matter, for the birth rate is affected by many factors other than family income. These factors appear when researchers compare one population group with another. The Growth of American Families study conducted in 1955 selected religion and level of education as the major factors influencing family size. The effect of income on family size appeared to be weaker than either education or religion.[64] A similar study conducted in 1960 confirmed these findings. The effect of religion has been summarized as follows:

Religion is a major factor in sculpturing completed family size. Religious fertility differentials—Catholics, high; Jews, low; with Protestants in between—appeared to be diminishing a decade ago, but recent studies indicate that since 1955 the traditional gap between Catholics and Protestants has widened again. It is unlikely that this trend will change even where economic and social differences between the groups are eliminated, because the greatest fertility differences often are found at the highest educational and income levels.[132]

So too education is an important "regulator" of fertility.[132] The more highly educated groups of the population have increased their average family size in each of the last several decades, moving toward the more stable averages of the poorly educated. Nevertheless, one thousand married women born in the late 1920's will, if they had less than an eighth-grade education, probably have between 3,600 and 3,900 children. Those who have completed college will probably have between 2,500 and 2,900 children.[27] Thus to some extent education seems to govern fertility.

If women work after marriage, the chances are that they will have fewer children. The evidence on this point is systematic and independent of family income.[62] It can only be attributed in part to the fact that women who cannot have children may choose to work. Presumably families postpone having children and in some cases avoid having additional children *in order to* make it possible for the women to work. In this sense family patterns that encourage women to work—increasingly widespread in the United States—are restraints on fertility. More central to our concerns here, an income maintenance program that permits or encourages mothers to work, as we have suggested a program should do in the case of mothers of school-age children, would tend to limit fertility.

Other factors affecting fertility should be mentioned. Rural families and city families with a rural background tend to have more children than average.[220, 45] With the continued movement to cities, the significance of this factor should diminish. It may be expected that housing policies affect family size.[50] In the last analysis the decision to have a child is made or evaded by people; styles in family size and other psychological factors must also play a role. Paul H. Douglas mentioned one kind of psychological factor in responding on one occasion to the claim that family allowances would cause an increase in population. He said:

There are other than economic barriers to large families. Children tax the endurance and patience of their mothers, and even were women assured that their children would be provided with sufficient food and clothing, few would wish to bring large families into the world.[43]

There speaks not a distinguished economist and professor but an attentive father.

Demographic developments that are in a sense accidental influence the number of births in a given year or decade. The baby boom after World War II will lead to a marriage boom during the late 1960's and a rise in total births shortly afterward. No real trend may be discernible, only the annoying human predilection for moving in fits and starts rather than in ideal curves. We have noted that people are marrying younger and having children earlier. Such trends produce a temporary rise in the annual birth rate; they may or may not affect the total number of children women have in a lifetime. We have also experienced an increase in the proportion of people who marry, leading to an increase in the birth rate per thousand population but not in births per family.

This catalogue of factors affecting the birth rate in the United States, though far from exhaustive, leads to a simple conclusion. We have already drawn a roughly similar conclusion from the experience of other countries. With care, researchers can distinguish a role that total income may play in increasing the short-term birth rate. Total personal income in the United States approximates $500 billion a year. A fair-sized new income maintenance program would probably constitute no more than 1 per cent of this amount. And total personal income is only one —and not the most powerful—item in our catalogue. The birth rate is compounded of income and one's conception of income, of education and ignorance, of conviction and faith, of geography and technology, of love and covetousness, of accident and design.

It does not seem that the overall birth rate would be markedly affected in the short run or affected at all in the long run by a new income maintenance program.

There remains the special problem of low-income families. We cannot be content if they are led to handicap themselves with large families, even if this development does not loom very large in national statistics. Concern about the relationship of poverty and family size arises from more or less overlapping bodies of information. First is the prevalence of poverty among large families. We have dwelt on the problem with respect to disorganized families. It may also occur in intact families. Young married women, through their early twenties, have fewer children if their husbands have a smaller income. College students, whose income is low and who postpone having children, must account somewhat for this tendency.* In any event, the older poor families surpass other families in number of children. For example, white mothers in their early forties average 3.6 children each if their husbands earned under $2,000 in 1959. Similar mothers, if their husbands earned over $5,000, averaged 2.7 children each.[202]

A second source of concern is a large number of studies that "document an inverse relationship between status measures and fertility." [62] Many of the explanations proffered for this relationship center about the consequences of upward mobility for families: better education, later marriage, and access to the best means of contraception may all lead to the having of fewer children. On the other hand, it is possible to view the relationship as a consequence of the determination to achieve improved status: like the heroic families mentioned in Chapter 3, ambitious families arrange to control births in order to achieve their ends. We have surmised that each view is partially correct.

---

* If one considers family rather than husband's income, fewer children are associated with *more* income, except in the youngest group of white wives, aged fifteen to nineteen. Presumably the woman who works because her husband earns little tends to have fewer children in the first years of marriage.[202]

A third source of concern is undoubtedly the body of observations about Negro family patterns. The low-income white mother mentioned above has 3.6 children, but a non-white mother at the same age and income level has five children. Negro families more commonly than white families show symptoms of disorganization—separation, illegitimacy. Breathes there a man educated beyond monosyllables who has not heard of the Negro matriarchal family? Much of the contrast between Negro and white family patterns—contrast of *average* behavior—reflects the far larger proportion of Negroes who are poor. How much difference, if any, may be attributed to factors other than poverty (discrimination, ethnic patterns) must, in the absence of relevant research, depend on judgment or bias.

Each stream of material in its own way establishes a connection between fertility and low income. We have explored at length what the nature of this connection may be. Poverty and large families may result from the same unfortunate circumstances—premature family and occupational choices, limited education and competence in general, limited resources. Poverty, family breakdown, and family size interact; year by year they contribute to one another. One can find in the relationship between low income and family size reason to believe that more income would lead to more children. One can also find reason to believe the opposite. Let us look at these reasons separately.

The poor education and relative incompetence of poor families will not immediately be altered by cash payments. Children may improve in these respects; some parents may further their education but many will not. It may be difficult to believe that families generally will seize on the prospect of an additional $25 or $50 a month deliberately to have an additional child. As Ronald Freedman observed, such a belief requires the conviction that poor families are now limiting the number of their children because they are miserable.[211] Nevertheless, it is plausible to assume that some uneducated families—from apathy, impulse, or

79

gratitude for the prospect of any cash income at all—may set out to have additional children. Whether the number will be large may be assessed in the light of the contrary argument.

The tendency of poor families to have somewhat more children might be altered in comparatively immediate, simple ways. The provision of adequate income might lead to the knowledge and materials that are needed for limiting family size. Especially may this be true with the development of oral contraceptives and the intra-uterine device, both apparently more acceptable than means previously used. Studies indicate that, when approached directly with birth control information, "large numbers" of low-income families take advantage of such measures.[37]

Beyond the simple response, the import of Chapter 3 is that the family-income cycle of poor families can be interrupted. Providing families with income with which to improve themselves is one method of altering family-income development. From this point of view, an adequate cash payment would lead out of poverty and act to limit family size as well. Although the argument from the family-income cycle is new, the argument that higher income will lead to smaller families is not. Joseph Willard has summarized it as follows:

> It can be argued . . . that as the income of the family unit is raised the birth rate will decline. Numerous studies have recorded differences in family size associated with differences in income and nearly all have led to similar conclusions, that the size of family becomes smaller as income rises and prosperity increases. It might be reasoned, therefore, that the addition of disposable income for the family . . . may sufficiently raise their standard of living so that they behave, after a time lag for adjustments, in accordance with social standards of typical persons at the new level rather than the old.[230]

The crux of this argument is an unknown. If people with lower incomes are provided with more money, will they become similar in their fertility patterns to people who have more money? Those who hesitate to answer "yes" are conscious that the question is complex. Is it partly because they have limited the number of their children that many people have a decent in-

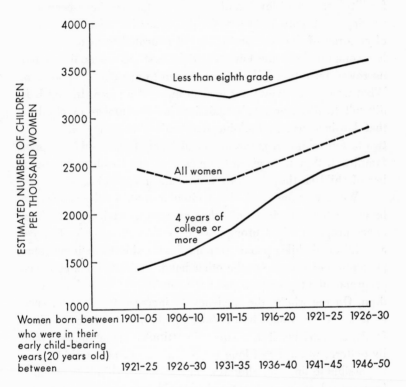

FIGURE 5–2. Estimated number of children per thousand white women, by women's educational attainments and dates of birth. Source: Arthur A. Campbell, "Recent Fertility Trends in the United States and Canada," paper presented at the World Population Conference, Belgrade, Yugoslavia, 1965. The women born between 1921 and 1930 have not necessarily completed child-bearing; "low" estimates of their fertility are used to provide completed figures. Figures are for all children of women who were married at least one.

come? If a disorganized family is simply provided with income, will family patterns be affected? Is money by itself so powerful? Perhaps accumulating data on the desires of low-income families contain a hint of what might happen. As Figure 5–2 shows, the fertility patterns of low- and high-income families have been converging. In twenty-five years the difference between the number of children of the least and the most educated women (more or less comparable to the lowest- and highest-income families) has narrowed from two children per woman to one child per woman. What women say they want is even more of a piece. In fact it is difficult to discover much variation in the number of children that low-income and high-income families say they want;[63, 148] two to four children is the universal ideal. Then would not poor families, if they were given the means, attempt to have the number of children they say they want—and no more?

We have come again by a circular route to the conclusion based on the experience of other countries. An income maintenance program might prompt some low-income families to have an additional child; people respond inscrutably to their personal perception of events. On the other hand, an income maintenance program might prompt some poor families to have fewer children. On the whole, the tendency to increase family size, such as it would be, would be of short range. The tendency to limit family size, arising from changes in attitude, education, and family pattern, would be of long range. In retrospect it would prove impossible to find any alteration in the relationship between low-income and other birth rates that could be attributed to a new income maintenance program.*

* Figure 5–2 provides an opportunity to test this point with regard to a large income maintenance program for children. Aid to Families with Dependent Children was introduced in 1935; its effects would have been felt by 1936 or 1937. Well-educated women who were in their early twenties in 1935 (and were presumably to be having children through the 1950's) were to average more children than comparable women five years earlier. Five years later, comparable women increased their family size even more sharply. In contrast, poorly educated women

It is only fair to note here the argument that an income maintenance program would increase births among families who have more income. As we have seen, births increased among French families with comfortable incomes concurrently with the development of family allowances. One French demographer argues, therefore, that family allowances increase the birth rate by permitting those who are interested in the future of their children —those with the fewest children and the highest status—to have additional children.[57] This point of view is lent support by an American study of family behavior with respect to fertility. The study concludes that there is "one central norm" about family size: "One should not have more children than one can support, but one should have as many children as one can afford." [148] Those who have deliberately limited the number of their children in keeping with their view of what they can afford—presumably middle-class families or those moving up—might, with a government payment, decide to have an additional child. Here again we must acknowledge the possibility that a program might lead to some number of additional children. In the same sense, however, increased national income may lead to more births among the same families. It is difficult to regard an income maintenance program as a substantial factor.

CONCLUSION

No rigorous scientific demonstration can be made that income maintenance will lead to a higher birth rate or that it will not.

in their early twenties in 1935 show a decline in average number of children from a comparable group five years earlier. Five years later, a comparable group records a small increase in average family size.

The point of this exercise is negative. The trends charted were probably in response to general economic improvement, to the onset of war, and other major forces. But one who seeks a relation between fertility and income maintenance finds, in the United States as in Canada, that the data are not merely uninformative but seem to move in the wrong direction.

One who desires to wait for scientific demonstration of either result before devising an income maintenance program must be prepared to wait a long time. Apart from the inherent difficulties of measurement, demographers who might direct such research have tacitly concluded that the answer is already evident. Other demographers may retain a willingness to be persuaded that substantial income would significantly increase fertility, at least for some types of families, but find more important matters to occupy their time.

In all probability, a new income maintenance program would lead some people, including some who are poor, to have additional children. But this effect would be trivial in relation to concurrent developments and would not be discernible in subsequent population figures. Balancing any small effect, a substantial income maintenance program should significantly improve the circumstances of many families. In their children's generation, at least, it may provide the competence and climate to achieve the family size that that generation will genuinely want.

II

INCOME
MAINTENANCE
PROGRAMS

✜✜✜✜✜✜✜✜✜✜✜✜✜✜✜✜✜✜✜✜

6

Purposes
and Issues

☨☨☨☨☨☨☨☨☨☨☨☨☨☨☨☨☨☨☨☨

We are not the first generation to con-
clude that we need no longer tolerate want. Governor Jeremiah
Smith told the New Hampshire Legislature over 150 years ago:
"That there should be legal provision for all the necessitous, it
is believed will be questioned by none." [98] But the context in

which we come to that conclusion and the content with which we carry it out may indeed be novel.

The United States was born in a libertarian era when the establishment of property rights freed men from feudalism. The United States, someone has said, "was born free." The battle of property rights is so well won as to be out of mind; now we hear more and more frequently of the need to establish human rights. The Civil Rights Act of 1964 asserted the importance of human over property rights. The nation gropes for ways to insure human dignity beyond the theoretical provision of opportunity. As R. H. Tawney wrote in 1938:

> [Equality of opportunity] was formulated as a lever to over-throw legal inequality and juristic privilege and from its infancy has been presented in negative, rather than positive, terms. It has been interpreted rather as freedom from restraints than as the possession of powers.[187]

Now, in a country that knows and has wealth, human rights are beginning to be seen as affirmative characteristics—not in terms of the absence of restraint or of want but as the possession of power to choose one's occupation, associations, ideals, and way of life.

This leads us to make one assumption that will guide us in evaluating income maintenance programs: We seek for children not simply sufficiency but power to make choices; this power rests on complex requirements and must be continuous. It requires not only laws to safeguard it, but also nutrition, education, and pride. If childhood has not been properly served, power cannot be conferred at majority.

A prior assumption should be noted. The primary objective of a national program is to prevent children from having insufficient goods and services. Sufficiency is not regarded as a fixed quality. A hundred years ago sufficiency was food, shelter, and clothing. We may now be in the process of adding cultural opportunities to the basic rights. Evidently sufficiency is not only objective or biological but is somehow tied to what the average person has at a given time. The point is borne out by a historic review of poverty. Did the Council of Economic Advisers judge a fifth of the population to be poor in 1964? In 1904, Robert Hunter estimated that 12 to 24 per cent of the population (10 to 20 million people) lived in poverty.[84] As Dorothy Brady has observed, "The same proportions of the population are found to be poor . . . in widely varying times and places." [103] Theodore Schultz suggests that, in the recent past at least, the amount of income that commonly defines poverty has increased at about half the rate of average income.[172]

It is not difficult to provide a rationale for the definition of poverty that will be used when average income has somewhat advanced over the next few years. We have noted that the Department of Agriculture's economy food budget, on which the official definition of poverty has been based, is for emergency use only. Side by side with its published estimates of the poor population based on the official definition, the Social Security Administration has provided a set of estimates based on the cost of providing "an adequate diet at low cost." [138, 139] Official use of such a budget in 1963 would have led to the conclusion that one third of American children are poor. So true an echo of Roosevelt's "one third of a nation" can hardly have been expected to be uttered. But when we adopt the low-cost budget in 1973, will we be surprised to learn that one fifth of American children are poor?

While we are in the process of wiping out poverty—as it was defined in 1963 and refined several times since—imperceptibly, but as certainly as watching a child grow, our very conception of poverty changes year by year. If we are to overleap the relativity of our conception of poverty, then, it cannot be only by modifying the absolute amounts of income that 15 million poor children receive but by modifying the *proportion of the*

89

total that they receive. Though some children may have more and some less, none may be quite as far below average as many children now are. The primary objective of assuring sufficiency incorporates a subsidiary objective: to provide a fairer share of national income to the families in which children now poor are living. The two objectives are compatible but not identical, especially in a growing economy. On the contrary, history records many occasions when highly touted programs for the poor masked the increasingly privileged position of those who had more.

It is assumed, third, that effectiveness in avoiding need is not the sole test by which to evaluate programs. We have dwelt with some care on the family cycle of poor children, in order to be able to ask how a program will affect the child's family and its development. This question is our second major test. A program's side effects are also of major significance. More than once we have prescribed a remedy for one problem, only to have it painfully borne in upon us that other problems were set in motion. To this day Aid to Families with Dependent Children can, in some states, readily lead fathers to desert families; and public housing makes institutional enclaves of large areas of our cities. It is saner to foresee side effects and to avoid them.

A final assumption must already be evident. We do not seek a makeshift measure. We seek a mechanism that will find ultimate though not necessarily impulsive acceptance from Americans, both in the moments when they view themselves as taxpayers and when they view themselves as beneficiaries.

In this chapter we shall deal with the issues that lead to specific types of income maintenance programs. From the starting point of childhood poverty we might easily move in other directions. We might dwell on opportunity programs, a generalized program of income maintenance, or public assistance. We might get caught up in a conflict perhaps more apparent than

real—the opposition between providing cash and providing services. The reader has a right to know why we are led to specified
alternatives; moreover, the argument will make explicit other assumptions than those already noted.

OPPORTUNITY PROGRAMS AND
INCOME MAINTENANCE

In moving directly to income maintenance to meet the problem
of childhood poverty, we bypass the programs designed to enhance a person's ability to make his own way in the world—
opportunity programs. The term usually refers to services that
can be visualized as contributing to earning power sooner or
later. The following observations would probably be generally
accepted.

Income maintenance is vital to opportunity programs; sick
or hungry children do not, in general, learn very well. Presumably a training program or special program for school dropouts
can incorporate its own subsistence grant. These programs are
not likely at any given moment, however, to be dealing with the
majority of poor children; and income maintenance cannot be con-
structed as a sporadic measure. In the end, opportunity programs
require employment. Sound programs will place more people
in jobs but, except in periods of crisis, substantial unemployment remains a fact of life. Nor, as we have noted, does employment obviate the problem for the growing number of children
who have no father. For these two groups, at least, mechanisms
other than opportunity programs are required.

Differences of opinion are likely to arise over practical
choices involving the expenditure of money. For example, the
Council of Economic Advisers offers the following advice on how
to organize the national attack on poverty.

91

Conquest of poverty is well within our power. About $11 billion a year would bring all poor families up to the $3,000 income level we have taken to be the minimum for a decent life . . . But this "solution" would leave untouched most of the roots of poverty. Americans want to *earn* the American standard of living by their own efforts and contributions. It will be far better, even if more difficult, to equip and to permit the poor of the Nation to produce and to earn the additional $11 billion, and more. We can surely afford greater generosity in relief of distress. But the major thrust of our campaign must be against cause rather than symptoms. We can afford the cost of that campaign too [Council's italics].[48]

The paragraph may seem repetitive but clearly an effort is being made to place measured emphasis on both sides of a potential conflict between income maintenance and the provision of opportunity. Efforts to enact great programs and mount them amidst contending forces inevitably entail a simplification of issues in which the emphasis is likely to be cruder and more one-sided. Especially is this so in the case of opportunity programs, which involve fewer people and more limited time spans and are likely to be cheaper. Moreover, as Harry Johnson has pointed out, it is tempting to administrators and intellectuals, who are themselves middle class, to believe that "elevation [from poverty] should be accomplished in ways consistent with middle-class morality"—that is, via education and hard work rather than simple transfers of income.[88]

Here it may be noted that children have a singular right to income maintenance. They are not responsible, whether or not their parents want or are able to use the opportunities we offer. And, while opportunity programs may conceivably benefit adults fairly rapidly, some children cannot benefit through their parents, and for themselves opportunity programs have a more remote pay-off. Children have a right to maintenance in the here and now.

Thus we observe two reasons for seeking an income maintenance program for children. First, opportunity programs must count on adequate income maintenance. Second, all children have a right to decent income maintenance at all times. At least as presently envisaged, opportunity programs cannot achieve this goal. It would be disarming to leave the matter at that and pass on; but an equally serious, if more complex and speculative, issue is also involved. In brief, we may be facing a choice between a more fluid society and one that is increasingly divided into compartments.

Sociologists have for many years been concerned with the forces in American society that have tended toward stratification —separation of people by class, ethnic group, and so forth. There have been differences of opinion, on theoretical grounds, as to how severe the separation was becoming. The closing of the frontier and the growing importance of education might tend to increase stratification by narrowing opportunity. Urbanization and mass communication might tend to diminish stratification by bringing people into closer contact with one another. Surveys have seemed to support the view that people's relationships are becoming highly "compartmentalized." An early study observed that:

> In short, a major trend in the social structure of the New Haven community during the last half-century has been the development of *parallel class structures* within the limits of race, ethnic origin, and religion [author's italics].[82]

We detect in this quotation the beginnings of a special emphasis. Early studies were concerned with movement up or down —financially or otherwise. Compartmentalization introduces the notion of separation between groups, even those more or less equal in status. In these senses, stratification is one kind of compartmentalization. The broader emphasis appears in a recent Detroit study of religious organizations. Its findings "force" consid-

93

eration of the possibility that American society is moving toward "a compartmentalized society," with social, economic, and religious distinctions separating groups from one another. A pluralistic society, the author points out, could come to be a euphemism for a compartmentalized society.[107]

Although obviously not the only forces involved, occupational and educational developments are important among the pressures that would segregate us into compartments. Diplomas are becoming vastly more important, not entirely for the learning they represent but because employers use them as a shibboleth. Even on-the-job training is being dominated by those with college educations.[125] We readily perceive the time when an advanced level of education will constitute "a necessary, but not a sufficient condition" for getting a job.[60] Personal connections become increasingly important. They have for many years been a primary means of securing work and advancement.[152, 213] Now we are witnessing the growth of certain professions (agent, consultant, lobbyist) that specialize in the sale of connections. A realm of "new property," including credentials bestowed by governments (the lowly driver's license, for example), influences one's occupation and associations.[151] One can imagine the development of a subtler guild system, dominated by exquisitely graded levels of achievement and name dropping (spoken and unspoken). Considerations of class, social origin, religion, education, and occupation will be represented and reinforced by credentials of varying types and significance. There will be little movement between compartments.

Opportunity programs are, in a certain sense, attempts to achieve entry to a guild for people who would otherwise be excluded. Indeed, when trainees are placed, it is not always clear whether to credit their better job performance or their possession of a formal document.[179, 178, 39] Therefore, opportunity programs emphasize the provision of credentials and, the more they are significant in society, lend impetus to the building of compartments. Moreover, in making their own selection of people to help, opportunity programs can only with great care avoid creating new guilds. To receive training at a specified level may require having had more primitive training. Selection processes inevitably involve judging whether the applicant is "feasible" for the objective. And any program administered by an organization favors people who are comfortable with and able to manipulate bureaucracies. A recurrent irony in dealing with poor people is that credentials (criteria, requirements), however selected, turn out to be overlapping ways of defining a comparatively privileged class.

Those who administer the programs are aware of these difficulties; but the existence of difficulties does not constitute a case against providing opportunity in every way possible. Nor should opportunity programs bear responsibility for the influence of influence; the truth is more nearly that they are an attempt to counteract it for at least some people. If we wish fluidity in our society, however, we will take pains to avoid *exclusive* reliance on mechanisms that require credentials and deepen their influence. For that reason, in dealing with childhood poverty, we must have a program that relies as little as possible on credentials: childhood—yes; some criterion of need—perhaps; diplomas or trainability—certainly not. This requirement causes us to look to income maintenance. The limited reach of opportunity programs as already noted is, of course, a more immediate and tangible spur.

CATEGORICAL OR GENERAL?

Assuming that we should have an income maintenance program, we face a second choice of direction. Where is it written that we must have a specific income maintenance program for children? Now that we have so many and such complicated income maintenance programs why should we not thoroughly reorganize so as to achieve one generalized system that would adequately include children?

The question is not an entirely new one. In the development of social security in the United States and western Europe the categorical approach has been deliberately chosen. A survey of European developments up to 1939 reported:

> The trend in the successive measures for the aid of the aged and other dependents has been toward increasing differentiation of the various types of destitution, and toward more adequate assistance for each group afforded principally through governmental action . . . The move toward more adequate aid for the needy went hand in hand with the development of "categorical" measures . . . The steps by which the western European countries proceeded from harsh and inadequate local poor relief laws to specialized old-age pension and insurance systems are broadly similar.[75]

Similarly the Committee on Economic Security observed that "a piecemeal approach is dictated by practical considerations." Speaking of children in particular, they were "strongly of the opinion that these families should be differentiated from the permanent dependents and unemployables." [34] Since the war western Europe has felt a push toward integration of social insurances, but categories of need have nevertheless been the dominant theme. In the United States old categories (the aged, the orphaned) have been expanded and new categories (the disabled) added.

Both political and functional considerations have led to a categorical approach in the United States. The proponents of each measure thought it easier to assemble the necessary consensus to enact a category than to reorganize social security. Unquestionably their political judgment was sound. The tendency has been to define even the categories quite narrowly in securing laws and to broaden them subsequently. It has also been thought that categories have advantages in principle. They focus upon particular groups in which the electorate is interested. For groups such as the aged that may universally require income, onerous tests of means or eligibility may be avoided.

Edith Abbott named several other reasons for adopting a categorical approach. In 1937 she set out to instruct her "eastern friends," who had said that categorical relief was "not approved."

> It is important [she said] that New York and the Middle West should understand each other—if possible. And, therefore, it is important that we should explain why we believe in providing special care for these various selected groups. First, because the people themselves prefer their public assistance that way. They would rather receive an old age pension, or mothers' aid, or unemployment benefit, or a blind pension, than to go on the general relief poor lists . . .
>
> A second reason . . . is that the new forms of public aid have provided more adequate and more stable grants than the old relief provided, and have avoided some, at least, of the humiliations of the old system.[2]

Although Miss Abbott was talking chiefly of public assistance, the arguments apply equally to social insurance. We have noted the contempt visited upon those who are thought to be getting a free ride. In order to avoid bringing such attitudes into play, the effort has been to tie each program to an acceptable unique quality (old age, widowhood, disability) rather than to their vexatious common quality (need).*

* The principle has application rather broader than the social insurances. The nation also makes money payments—without noticeable stigma—to categories of businesses defined as having special rights (farmers, protected industries, central city construction firms). Referring to these payments, Michael Harrington has now and then observed that Americans believe in socialism for the rich, just not for the poor.

97

It is difficult to know where we stand at this particular moment. Proposals have been made to replace the entire complicated present system with a single program operated in conjunction with the income tax. Such a proposal was made by Lewis Meriam in 1946.[119] He, like others, proposed not only to generalize current programs but to establish a lower level of income maintenance. On the other hand, those who intend a general program at levels that might be regarded as adequate might achieve not only simpler administration but also a system in which credentials play a very small role indeed. One wonders whether we may be coming to what Eveline Burns has called the third stage in the development of social insurance: "general acceptance of the doctrine of public, non-means tested, assurance of minimum income for all." [22] If this were so, two important changes would have to take place: first, that we should be able to legislate in this field much more broadly than we ever have; and second, that we should be able to concede to others and to feel for ourselves the right to a minimum income, without regard to criteria such as age. Dr. Burns writes that she doubts we have come to this stage.[22]

Meanwhile, even if one assumes that a generalized program is preferable, it would seem unfair to children to engage their fates in an uncertain movement to win such a program. For virtually all population groups (aged, widowed, disabled, unemployed) Congress has now established a fundamental mechanism that may be used to avoid poverty. The programs may have to be broadened or improved; Congress has only to take such steps when it sees the need and occasion. Children are the single population group for whom there is not, even in principle, a program of social insurance. (Survivors' benefits are available, to be sure, but most needy children suffer from other risks.) Development of a categorical program for children will put them on the same footing as all the rest.

In public debate in the 1960's the concept of a generalized

program has somewhat diffusely been represented by the term "guaranteed minimum income." Dr. Burns's definition—"minimum [income] to all as a matter of course and without regard to need" [22]—is a more precise meaning of the term. The argument for a categorical program leads us not to consider a guaranteed income in the exact terms of Dr. Burns's definition. We concluded in Chapter 4 that work will be the major source of family income for some time. Although we do not believe that a program without a means test is likely to sap incentive, it is difficult to conceive of Congress mounting a substantial general income guarantee while work is or is thought to be obligatory. Secondly we have asserted that children have a right to a categorical program like all the rest, until such time as the nation provides a general guarantee.

The term "guaranteed minimum income" has also been used in other senses. For instance, a demogrant is a payment without income test, for the whole population or limited only by age. When we consider a demogrant limited to children—that is, a family allowance—we avoid the problem connected with a general guarantee. The public is less likely to feel that income from work should be the sole or pre-eminent answer. Similarly the term "minimum income guarantee" has included programs that make payments *because* income is otherwise inadequate. In particular, the negative income tax has been proposed and we shall be giving it consideration. Robert Theobald uses "minimum income guarantee" to emphasize his plan to meet 100 per cent of the deficit, which many negative income tax proposals do not do.[190]

In short, in a very broad sense of the term, any gain in income maintenance represents a move toward a guaranteed income. In the precise sense of the term, only a generalized payment to all, without an income test, performs the task. In our view the United States has deliberately moved in other directions for many years and is not likely to alter its course until it takes a radically different view of work. The concept of a guaranteed income may be applied, with only slight blurring, to a demogrant such as a family allowance. A combination of such categorical payments might, through thoughtful combination, guarantee income to all groups who could not be expected genuinely to earn their own income. On the whole, such accretion appears to be the course the United States has followed so far. A certain conservatism in our estimate of the likelihood of change in this policy and our special concern for children lead us to explore further along the road of accretion.

SOCIAL INSURANCE OR ASSISTANCE?

Assuming that we should have a categorical income maintenance program, why should we seek a new program? One out of six children reaching adulthood in the 1960's has received Aid to Families with Dependent Children (AFDC) for some period of time.[130] The magnitude of this state-federal public assistance program reflects the scarcity of other income protections for children. Presumably it could be extended and strengthened to sustain all needy children. Why should we not move in *this* direction? From its enactment, AFDC has been regarded as spreading a safety net below children who escape other protections (survivors' insurance, unemployment compensation). There are reasons why it should remain a safety net with other protections for children arrayed above it. These reasons have to do with the means test and the state-federal system of financing the program.

A means test is a periodic demonstration that the resources available to a family will not be enough to provide defined needs —clothing, shelter, and so on. The gap between resources and needs, totted up in dollars and cents, is theoretically filled to provide a minimum income. The principle appears simple and almost inevitable, but as it is applied in large-scale programs it creates painful problems.

First, the family's incentive to produce income is undermined. Most families who need AFDC are unable to produce more than a few dollars a week from their own efforts. The father who has deserted has a new family to support; no court will require more than a small contribution from him. The mother may work, but she is unskilled and her children limit her time, her mobility, and her dependability. Thus the average contribution from a separated father to an AFDC family is about $7 a month, and the average income from all other sources, omitting social security, is less than $5 a month.[212] Consequently to expect many families to acquire an income substantially higher than the one they receive in assistance is unrealistic. But within the small income that is feasible, the means test operates to take away in assistance what the family secures by its own efforts. The law now permits states to disregard a certain amount of the family's income in establishing its payment. However, this merely shifts the level at which a family finds no further incentive to earn; it does not eliminate the problem. Moreover, few states have availed themselves of this liberalizing provision.

Second, the means test is expensive, requiring a small army of investigators to administer it. The number of positions for social workers in public assistance exceeds fifty thousand; the thousand nooks and crannies of the means test occupy most of their time. The State of New York spent $1.5 million in one year on one important cranny of the means test alone—determining the ability of adult children to support a needy parent.[206] There is a desperate shortage of personnel in all the helping professions. The fifty thousand in public assistance are, more usually than not, taxed beyond their capacity for offering the simplest advice and aid. It does not seem reasonable to select a program that will multiply the number of investigators required.

Third, although the appropriations involved in AFDC are large, the sums each family receives are modest—say, $125 a month. The adjustments made in the monthly payment—as women earn a little from housework, as children have birthdays, as relatives move in and out of the home—are from a public point of view trivial. For example, in the state of Colorado, seven out of ten payments change in a given month, with an average change of less than $3.[91] The picture of public officials negotiating with our poorest citizens in these matters day after day is not an attractive one. Officials quite often find themselves enforcing honesty and obedience to the law upon people who have the best reason for evading it—want. Obviously the law must be observed. But a great and wealthy country does not choose this sort of theater in which to enact its morality plays if there is a sound alternative.

The state-federal relationship in AFDC presents another set of problems. Without doubt the partnership offers administration of the program closer to where recipients live. But it also attunes coverage and standards of assistance to the wealth of each particular state. Two deadly problems are created. First, no matter how small the percentage a state is asked to contribute, the poorest states have difficulty in paying it. Indeed by measures of fiscal effort some of the poorest states make the greatest effort to support public services. Yet their public assistance programs tend to be the most inadequate.[3] What are their choices? Raising tax rates would put an undue burden on residents and discourage new industry. Spending less on *other* public services would mean sacrificing some program. Education? Public roads? What can be spared?

It is theoretically possible to eliminate the state's share of the cost entirely and continue state administration of the program. Even so, a second problem arises: budget standards would tend to be set in relation to the degree of poverty endemic within the state. In 1963 a family of three children and a mother in the median state required a minimum income of $203 a month. But such a family could receive no more than $97 on the average in the ten states with the highest proportion of poor families (under

$2,000 a year). Budget standards in the ten states were lower; regardless of standards, no more than a maximum payment was permitted.

Doubtless the cost of living was somewhat less in these states, but generalized poverty was the more powerful cause of low payments. The dilemma that arises in this situation is not easily resolved. People earning $2,000 or $3,000 do not readily set that amount as a public assistance standard. If they do, are they not reducing recipients' incentive to work? Does the state not subsidize employers who pay low wages? But if assistance is grossly inadequate, can children grow up well, alert, and educated? It is almost hopeless to try to resolve this dilemma within the framework of each particular poor state. The nation, with its larger resources and less concentrated poverty, may set standards that seem, from all points of view, realistic.

We have scanned five fundamental problems that arise under programs of public assistance. A means test by its nature creates a problem of incentive, causes an enforcement problem concerning trivial amounts of money, and is expensive (in money and personnel) to administer. A federal-state program of income maintenance presents a financial problem for those states least able to meet it. In the poorest states the very prevalence of poverty pulls the concept of an adequate budget below amounts that can, in a national sense, be regarded as decent. It is possible to devise improvements or corrections at each of these points.

In 1964 the Commissioner of Welfare proposed several corrective steps. Commenting on a review of the eligibility of AFDC recipients, the commissioner, Dr. Ellen Winston, said:

> The giving of financial assistance must be depersonalized if we truly believe in the right to needed aid. The conditions and procedures for providing it must be simplified. The adequacy of the amounts must be improved . . . The AFDC review confirmed the importance of building more incentives into public welfare programs . . .[232]

103

Elsewhere Dr. Winston proposed "that we must establish a national floor under public assistance payments." [231] These are not detailed proposals but they call for action, within the context of public assistance, on the problems of incentive, expensive administration, and adequacy of payments. In the process the problem of enforcement might also be dealt with; only the problem of state resources is not noted in these two particular statements. A national Advisory Council on Public Welfare later outlined a framework for dealing with these problems, including federal support of programs beyond levels that states can afford. It is apparent that one could start with the problems named and build an improved program. It may be stipulated that this requires to be done in any case.

There are several reasons why it is also useful to start afresh to define and evaluate new types of programs. First, proceeding via an existing program may narrow the range of possibilities to be considered. The question of desirability may yield to historical and practical questions. What is the intent of the existing program? What would states permit? Second, ideas that have appeared in the United States and other ideas that have been tried elsewhere deserve consideration on their own merits. One might be led to consider them in terms of improving a current program, but one might not. Third, the safety net concept has advantages of its own. Short of perfection, we require a back-up program that does for children (and others) what the best mechanisms we can devise somehow fail to do. Having such a program as AFDC frees us from sacrificing every other consideration in order to achieve universal coverage. The widest coverage is naturally desirable but such considerations as level of payment are equally important.

For these reasons we shall seek a new program for children. One new program, the negative income tax, may not seem entirely dissimilar to public assistance. Those who prefer may regard it—or one or more of its provisions—as a next step in the development of AFDC. No proposal is available that obviates the need

104

for AFDC. With a new program and above all without one, we require for children as strong and modern a program of AFDC as imagination and resources may call forth.

PUBLIC SERVICE
AND CASH PAYMENTS

A public policy seeking to assure minimum goods and services may in principle be achieved by providing those services directly or by providing cash to buy them. The United States has seemed to move at times in one direction and then the other. So far as poor people were concerned, the provision of things* (food, vouchers for clothing, poorhouses) was a recognized practice in the seventeenth century. In the last hundred years or so we have undertaken to provide free public education to all children, regardless of need. The Social Security Act, moving in the other direction, originally prescribed that states should provide public assistance in cash. During the depression the nation had come to feel that food vouchers and rent payments were humiliating and represented undue interference in people's affairs. Social insurance payments have also operated only through cash payments to beneficiaries—with the major recent exception of health insurance payments.

If one views public services and cash as competitive types of programs, it is not easy to discern a consistent principle operating in the choices we have made. Free public education reflected a depth of conviction about children and education at a time when

* In this discussion the term "public services" is used to include services organized by government, the usual meaning of the term, and also giving in kind (a surplus food program) and paying the seller on behalf of the client (as in vouchers for clothing or vendor payments for medical care). These practices contain qualitative differences and should not ordinarily be confused. They are combined here only in order to contrast them all with the type of program that provides a cash payment to be used at the discretion of the beneficiary.

105

all communities had disposable land. The subsequent balance of the interests of immigrant and religious groups in urban centers produced, in the mid-nineteenth century, a crucial consensus about the need for public education. Surplus commodity programs have, at least at times, simply reflected the fact that there were farm surpluses. Medical care has been provided as a public service—in municipal and veterans' hospitals and through public assistance—by a system of reimbursing hospitals and doctors or by hiring them. This method represents a simple response to the difficulties encountered in handling a medical program in any other way. Medical care may be occasional and very expensive. An unconditional payment to the patient would therefore pose all sorts of practical problems.

Although we cannot discern a historic principle, we must weigh advantages and disadvantages, for it is certainly possible to develop a new program around public services. A non-cash program can readily be devised so as to reach precisely those children who are needy and to waste relatively little on others. For example, it may be assumed that child health clinics in slum neighborhoods reach those families who specifically need their services and no others. Consequently a non-cash program can be comparatively inexpensive. Put another way, non-cash programs may provide the most to those children who need them, within the limits of available funds. This advantage is shared with cash-payment programs that are limited to people defined as needy. If a program of public services is made widely available, however, without an income limitation, it has no advantage of economy or specificity. As Alva Myrdal wrote:

> It must be admitted . . . that while emphasis on the colossal costs [of cash payments] is politically impressive, it is not a particularly valid argument. Whatever the method employed, children must be supported. Costs may not be considered increased if they are merely transferred from the individual fam-

106

ily to the public as a whole. Also reforms in kind will show huge cost items on the national budget. The only crucial question becomes one of waste or economy. The two alternative principles for redistributional reforms, in cash or in kind, therefore have to be compared as to their effectiveness in relation to financial outlays.[131]

In other words, the point of economy must be argued in terms of effectiveness rather than by simply trying to compare cash outlays. It has been said that a program of public services assures those effects that are publicly desired. In other words, certain items of consumption are publicly defined as essential and visibly reach children. With sufficient investment, any level of living for children may be assured; but this is an advantage only if one thinks cash payments less likely to achieve the same objective. This aspect of the question has come into focus in a number of countries as they debated programs of family allowances. Opponents of family allowances have thought children would not benefit; proponents thought they would. After it enacted its program, Canada attempted in a number of ways to determine the fact of the matter. The studies were muddied by the usual problems: How to separate the results of the new allowance from a general rise in the standard of living? How to separate out expenditures on children from family expenditures? The weight of the evidence seems to be that children benefited rather directly.[216, 115] After the program had been operating for about a decade, no one bothered to make such studies any more. The issue no longer commanded any interest in Canada.

It appears that cash payments may as easily assure a desired standard of living to children as public services in the case of those items that are readily purchasable. The matter may be different, however, with items of consumption that are not organized in the private market to meet universal or low-income demand. It might have been impossible, for example, to provide universal public education through cash payments to families so that they could purchase education. Put in these terms, the issue of effectiveness fades into an issue of practical organization. If services are intended to reach certain kinds of children, they have to be organized in a form that will be accessible to the children—in some cases, as public services.

The qualitative question of the impact of cash versus noncash programs tends to overlap with a demographic issue. In the classical Swedish debate on family policy of the 1930's, there was interest as to whether one type of program or the other would be more likely to increase the birth rate. The point was put in brief that payment in "cash favors quantity; kind favors quality." [131] That is, a cash payment would go to parents and act as an incentive to increasing the number of children. Services to children would improve their nutrition, health, and so forth but would not increase their number. This issue requires consideration as a separate matter (see Chapter 5). Here it is only necessary to bear in mind that a somewhat different argument is involved. The argument of economy is a general assertion that public services visibly produce desired results. The argument of quality versus quantity emphasizes a concrete illustration—the desire to avoid increasing the birth rate. It is well known that the Swedish people found themselves persuaded by these arguments; a variety of government commissions and citizen bodies rejected payments in cash. It is less widely known that an extensive program of cash payments was subsequently enacted, side by side with a wide program of public services for families. Thus on this issue Sweden has a mixed public policy.

In fact, no developed country moves solely in one direction or the other. Great Britain offers two conspicuous nationwide services—public housing, with rents well below actual cost, and the National Health Service—but an extensive system of cash payments to meet other needs. Several Scandinavian countries provide vacations, homemakers, and special child-care facilities; they also provide cash payments for children. One may wonder whether the opposition between cash and public service programs is more semantic than actual. No one proposes a package of non-cash services and the elimination of cash programs, or vice versa. Rather, the issue is *what mix* of public services and cash payments to have. More specifically, what items shall we from time to time extract from the array of expenditures paid out of private family budgets in order to provide them through public services?

In these terms we may discern several overlapping factors that seem to lead to benefits in kind. First, we judge by the item's significance to the nation as a whole: some things are so important to the nation that we do not leave them to individual choice. Second, we judge on the basis of economy or effective organization. Third, we judge from our developing view of what things all individuals are entitled to have that may, fourth, be comparatively difficult for their own families to provide. For example, viewing the future also within the context of children's needs, Alfred J. Kahn proposes the simultaneous development of broader income maintenance and what he calls social utilities. "Social utility" is a term for public services that emphasizes the sense of common need and universal availability. Kahn foresees the development of social utilities such as beginners' day schools and school lunch programs, home helps and "park aunts" (playground baby-sitters), family and child vacations, and citizens' advice bureaus.[92]

Education and the public services more commonly taken for granted (police, public roads) meet several of the criteria listed for a public service. So too may medical care, in particular medical care for poor children. Because of its strategic situation, education may increasingly serve as the nucleus around which other programs of public service for children are organized: school lunch, school health, tutoring, recreational and cultural programs, and so forth.

It has been pointed out that there are dangers in thinking only of criteria that lead to public services. We do not wish without good reason or in too large degree to infringe upon the freedom that cash gives a person to select his way of life. Three cautions have therefore been formulated. First, public services should not substitute for cash "where the latter is more appropriate." For example, a food stamp program may have the untoward effect of depressing cash payments in public assistance. Second, public services should be available in a fashion that distributes them equitably. Objective criteria of eligibility have so far been more successfully developed in relation to cash than social services. Finally, public services should not be used "as an instrument of social control" of groups such as Negroes, unmarried mothers, or fathers refusing work relief assignments.[223]

Viewing in terms of the four factors that seem to lead to public services and of the three cautions that confine them, we can hardly conceive of all children's needs being met by programs of public service. Especially if we view minimum needs as a constantly changing quantum, especially if we view children's rights as affirmative power rather than minimum subsistence, we require a program that is able to expand. This was put as follows by Hope Eldridge:

> There is an aspect of human aspiration that should not be forgotten, namely, its indefinite expansibility. The fruits of progress are readily taken for granted and concepts of "needs" can reform again and again. . . . It is this aspect, perhaps, that makes the case for cash allowances.[50]

We see public services as part of the package that the nation, basing its mixture on expediency and principle, provides for children. Public services are, by their nature, likely to represent some but not all widely accepted elements of need. Income maintenance must provide the rest.

CONCLUSION

We seek a program that prevents need among children. In achieving this, it will tend to give a larger share of national goods and services to those children now poor. It will not have side effects that injure them; it should indeed provide money in ways and at times that may alter their life chances. We seek a mechanism that, whatever the initial reactions to it, will seem in one decade or two to have been natural and irreplaceable. Approaches other than income maintenance play a part in what must be done for children, but none replaces what income maintenance may do. We therefore consider three potential programs of income maintenance for children.

7

Fatherless Child Insurance

†††††††††††††††††††††

We begin with fatherless child insurance, the program that most nearly follows the traditional pattern of development of social security.

We have teased out some of the tangled threads that connect family breakdown and poverty. Marital difficulty and low income are tied together like partners in a neurotic marriage. No one can say which started the trouble but, once started, problems feed back and forth between the partners. Two proportions will highlight a point that is already in our minds: Two thirds of the children in families headed by women are poor by the definition we are using.[138] Lone mothers with children have, on the average, two fifths of the income of married couples.[136] In Chapter 3 we saw reasons to suspect that the income problem of socially orphaned children may persist even when they gain a stepfather.

In short, except that its origins seem today rather more social than economic, the risk to a child of being socially orphaned contains the very elements that have historically led us to social insurance: (1) The risk is built into our social structure and the injured person (the child) has no control over it. (2) More often than not, it leads to insufficient income. (3) All citizens must regard themselves as having been subject to the risk. (4) Protection, although feasible through risk-sharing (social insurance), can virtually not be provided by solitary planning. (5) This risk is probably the most important of those for which we have not so far attempted social insurance.[171]

The 1960 census counted 3 million children living with a parent who was divorced or separated. (For various reasons the number is probably a substantial understatement.) Many of these parents will marry or remarry; obviously the situation of some children is temporary. We may assume that the chances of marriage, legal or de facto, diminish markedly from the age of thirty on. Reasoning conservatively from this premise, we can say that 2 million of the 3 million children are permanently socially orphaned. If a new program dealt with no more than these 2 million children, it would have the impact of the social security program that now protects orphaned children.

Approaching the problem as an insurable risk, then, we may define fatherless child insurance (FCI) as social insurance protection for children against the loss of a parent for a reason other than death. (Some of the children involved are *motherless*, but

113

never mind.) The basic principle appeared in the Beveridge Report in the following terms:

> Divorce, legal separation, desertion and voluntary separation may cause needs similar to those caused by widowhood. They differ from widowhood in two respects: that they may occur through the fault or with the consent of the wife, and that except where they occur through the fault of the wife they leave the husband's liability for maintenance unchanged. If they are regarded from the point of view of the husband, they may not appear to be insurable risks; a man cannot insure against events which occur only through his fault or with his consent, and if they occur through the fault or with the consent of the wife she should not have a claim to benefit. But from the point of view of the woman, loss of her maintenance as housewife without her consent and not through her fault, is one of the risks of marriage against which she should be insured; she should not depend on assistance. Recognition of housewives as a distinct insurance class, performing necessary service not for pay, implies that, if the marriage ends otherwise than by widowhood, she is entitled to the same provision as for widowhood, unless the marriage maintenance has ended through her fault or voluntary action without just cause. That is to say . . . she should get temporary separation benefit (on the same lines as widow's benefit), and guardian or training benefit where appropriate.[11]

The Beveridge Report recommendation emphasized the problem of the lone woman rather than that of her children. Lord Beveridge assumed, incorrectly as it turned out, that the family allowance would be sufficient in amount to meet the needs of children. In any event, the report proposed to apply the insurance principle to certain cases of divorce and separation. More recently in England the idea has been revived in a book called *Fatherless Families*[235] and christened "fatherless child allowance." In the United States application of the insurance principle to the needs of socially orphaned children was suggested in 1960 by an Advisory

Committee to the Commissioner of Social Security.[176] It has never been discussed here in a painstaking or sustained fashion, however.

Only Australia and New Zealand provide payments in accordance with this general approach. Benefits are paid to deserted, separated, and divorced wives under the general provisions for widows. A special procedure assures that separation is involuntary, from the woman's point of view, or justifiable. Support provided by a husband is deducted from the benefit. In all other ways a separated or divorced woman receives the treatment accorded a widow. In New Zealand a deserted woman with one child receives about $1,200 a year (plus a $109 family allowance). A deserted woman with six children receives $1,565 a year (plus a $655 family allowance). If the divorced woman has other income exceeding $728 a year, the benefit is reduced by the amount of the surplus.

PROPOSAL

Let us consider the following proposal for the United States. Children deprived of a parent because of divorce or legal separation would receive benefits under the general conditions and scale of payments that apply to survivors' insurance. Application would be made by the parent who cares for them. However, a parent found guilty of an illegal act in connection with the divorce or legal separation could not receive benefits.

Applicants would be expected to take steps to secure support appropriate to the children's need and the father's income. Support payments under court order would not be mixed with benefit payments under the program. If the court-ordered support payment is larger than the benefit, the mother would naturally have the option of accepting it and withdrawing her application for benefits. If the benefit payment is the larger of the two and the mother accepts it, support ordered by a court would be paid into specially established funds. These funds would be used in each state for preventing family breakdown and for legal assistance in particular. As with other social security programs, FCI would be financed through employee and employer contributions based on wages.

These specifications are based on the following considerations. The contingency that entitles a parent to a benefit cannot lie completely within her control. Some process must establish that the marriage has not been dissolved for trivial reasons or in order to obtain an insurance payment. The courts are generally entrusted with weighing public against private interest and are in any case the appropriate agency for terminating a marriage. Therefore, eligibility must be limited to those whose marriage has been terminated *in a court*. Depending upon the state, to obtain a divorce may require the finding that one party is legally guilty— of adultery, for example. Conviction for an offense cannot reasonably become the basis for awarding a benefit; therefore the exclusion of guilty parents. Since couples usually select the least unpleasant grounds for divorce available under state law, however, the number affected by excluding guilty parents would probably be small.

Although many fathers may be unable to support their children, the public interest must be represented in the making of this decision. The matter might be dealt with administratively. However, all beneficiaries of the proposed program would be coming into court anyway, and it seems proper that the court should rule on support. At first thought one might wish to see support payments applied to reducing the child's benefit or refunded to the government as partial repayment. But this would create an endless series of administrative problems: adjustment of benefit payments to accord with whether or not a father had met his obligation; timing federal payments to coincide with county or state court orders and periodic changes of them; securing county or state court cooperation in collecting numerous but comparatively small amounts of money for the federal program. The proposal therefore provides, in effect, that a county or state court would order and oversee payments into a state fund. If a mother prefers to accept a support payment instead of a benefit, presumably because the support payment is larger, the matter is between her and the father and no government program intervenes. The preceding observations refer to support ordered by a court. Voluntary additional payments by the father would not affect the benefit in any way.

As legal action connected with divorce and support may be complicated or expensive, many families might require attorneys without payment or at reduced fees. Special state funds established with receipts from court-ordered payments would be used to support free access to the courts for poor people as well as other desirable measures relevant to family breakdown—the risk with which the program deals.

The conditions under which survivors' insurance is normally paid should be borne in mind: The mother's benefit ends if she remarries and may end or be reduced if she earns over $1,500 a year. Regardless of the mother's earnings, the children's benefit continues until they are eighteen (or twenty-two, if in school), but ends if they marry or are legally adopted. Benefits vary, depending on the wage record of the father. The minimum benefit payable, regardless of the father's prior earnings, is $33 a month for the mother and the same amount for each child.

HOW MANY WOULD BE COVERED?

Potential beneficiaries may be estimated at 4.7 million children (1963), of whom 4.2 million are from families that were divorced and 500,000 from families that were legally separated.* As many

* The estimate contains unavoidable uncertainties. It rests, first, on the assump-

117

as half a million children might turn out not actually to have coverage,* leaving 4.2 million children in something less than 2 million families receiving benefits. The cost of the program might be about $4 billion.

Although 4.2 million children is a respectable number of children—almost as many as are now covered by survivors' insurance and AFDC together—it represents only a little more than a fourth of all needy children. Moreover, not all 4.2 million are poor. About half of the children live in families in which the divorced parent has remarried.† All indications are that, on the average, remarried families have a lower income than families

---

tion that of the children whose parents had divorced in the eighteen years prior to 1963, 60 per cent were living and less than eighteen years old in 1963. Estimates available in *American Marriage and Divorce*[86] and from the Division of Vital Statistics, National Center for Health Statistics, give a total of seven million children of parents divorced in the preceding eighteen years. Thus 4.2 million children of divorced parents are regarded as still under eighteen. Second, it is assumed on very slight evidence that a third of the children living with a separated parent (1.6 million children in 1960) represents the number of children involved in separations that are legal or that could, for purposes of obtaining a benefit, readily be made legal.

* In order to be covered, a child's parent must be "fully" or "currently" insured. Currently insured status would probably usually be invoked; it requires six quarters (1½ years) of work covered by social security during the thirteen quarters preceding the death, retirement, disability, or, in this case, divorce or legal separation.

† An estimate of the proportion of children living with a remarried parent is provided from 1960 data. From the same sources as formed a basis for the calculation of potential beneficiaries, it is estimated that 3.8 million children of parents who had been divorced were living and under eighteen in 1960. Paul Glick estimates, on the basis of census reports and unpublished computations, that in that year 1.7 million children of divorced parents lived in various situations other than remarriage (i.e., with one divorced parent, with neither parent, with a parent who remarried but then became widowed, etc.). The remaining 2.1 million must have been living in the home of a parent who was remarried. The 500,000 children whose parents are legally separated obviously cannot be with a parent who has remarried. In short, in 1960, 2.2 million children of divorce and legal separation (1.7 million plus .5 million) were living with one parent or with neither and 2.1 million children were living with a parent who was remarried. (See "Marriage Instability: Variations by Size of Place and Region." [71])

that never separate. That is not to say that they are poor. The child living with a remarried parent may acquire new brothers and sisters. If remarriage places children in a situation in which they have less need of a benefit, at the same time the benefit protects the standard of living of their new brothers and sisters. The other half of the children who would be covered are in families headed by women or are living with neither parent. About their need we have already been sufficiently clear.

The impact of the program could be visualized if we could show the degree of poverty suffered by the children who would be covered. Unfortunately a clear demonstration of this sort requires data that have never been gathered—the income of children in families in which a parent has been divorced or the earnings history of divorced fathers. We may at least illustrate the impact by describing the income, in relation to the poverty level, of families receiving survivors' insurance. (See Table 7–1.)

It is apparent from Table 7–1 that, among the families who receive the lowest benefits, those with three or more children do not escape poverty by receiving survivors' insurance, nor would they do so with fatherless child insurance. The problem of large families directly reflects a regulation governing survivors' insurance: The maximum family benefit based on very low earnings is only twice the minimum benefit per person—$33. Thus the mother with one child, if she barely attains coverage, receives 40 per cent of her minimum needs; additional children mean only an additional deficit. The problem would be more acute in the case of fatherless child insurance than in survivors' insurance. Divorce and separation tend to strike early in marriage and death strikes later. Comparatively more children might therefore become socially orphaned while their fathers' earnings were still low.* In addition to the children in large families, some children receiving low benefits in small families are poor. Some children receiving

---

* To be sure, entirely apart from FCI, this aspect of maximum benefits ought to be reconsidered.

119

TABLE 7-1. *Total Income of Mothers and Children Receiving Survivors' Insurance, by Number of Children in Family, 1962*

MEDIAN TOTAL INCOME	MOTHER AND ONE CHILD	MOTHER AND TWO CHILDREN	MOTHER AND THREE OR MORE CHILDREN
Of families with highest benefits (34 per cent of the children)	$3,760	$4,670	$4,660
Of families with median benefits (34 per cent of the children)	2,960	3,640	4,080
Of families with lowest benefits (31 per cent of the children)	2,760	2,670	2,340
Poverty level [a]	1,990	2,440	3,685

Source: U. S. Department of Health, Education, and Welfare. *Widows with Children under Social Security.*[210] In press.

[a] For simplicity, the same level is used here as elsewhere in the study. As the income concerns units in which there is only one adult, lower and slightly more accurate amounts might have been provided. The average number of children in the families of three or more children is 3.9. Therefore, the poverty level used in that column applies to four children and an adult.

higher benefits are also poor, if their families have no income in addition to the benefits. In sum, almost one third of the children receiving survivors' insurance—preponderantly in families with three or more children—are poor despite the payments.[210]

For the other two thirds of the children, matters look better. The average survivors' benefit (in 1963, $1,673 to $2,310, depending on family size) takes a family a long way toward the poverty level. If there is income of any other sort (savings, commercial insurance, earnings), the family lives neither in nor at the edge of poverty but presumably with a sense of sufficiency

and security. It is an experience for children that is much to be
desired.

IS TAKE-OFF POSSIBLE?

Fatherless child insurance is addressed only to the need of children
who are socially orphaned. Consequently it offers nothing to poor
families at the crucial point of marriage and first vocational
choice. One may say either that the program is irrelevant at this
stage or that it fails at this stage, as one chooses. As a legally dissolved marriage is a requirement for benefits, illegitimate children
are not eligible under the proposal. But the program has relevance
for women who are unmarried and pregnant for they may see in
it a reason to regularize their relationship. Youths face the decision whether to make a forced marriage with considerable ambivalence. Both the young man and the young woman, we have
noted, are influenced in making their decision by practical considerations such as income. The notion that a benefit will be provided for the child if the marriage fails—as they may expect—
cannot help but tip some toward attempting marriage.

However marriages begin, hesitation and vacillation attend
marital difficulty, and inevitably court action itself requires time.
Delays of a year or two are therefore likely to take place between
the actual onset of need and the start of benefit payments. Moreover, one can imagine that the youngest parents, having not yet
achieved one and a half years of covered employment, would postpone suit for divorce or legal separation. Seen as encouraging an
earnest test of the possibilities of a sound marriage, these delays
can only be accepted or approved. But seen in relation to the
unmet needs of mothers and children, such delays must be regarded as a drawback.

If fatherless child insurance fails to help prevent the first

121

mistakes, so to speak, it may give some young families a second try. We noted that early pregnancy or marriage is, in a certain sense, a form of family cycle squeeze. With her marriage failing, the young woman faces choices about work and child care. The young man may be required to furnish support when he should instead be returning to school or undergoing some sort of training. The support order, if the amount is large enough to support the woman and child reasonably, may cause the man to return home[94] —presumably only to leave again at the next disagreement. As for the woman, if lonely and sufficiently needy, she may accept the next man who promises her a few dollars or clothes for her child.[142] All these choices tend to lead to poverty.

The introduction of even a minimum benefit ($66 a month) might ease the situation considerably. An average benefit ($140 a month for a mother with one child, $193 for a mother with two children) virtually assures minimum living conditions for a family at this stage. The woman would be able to make choices based on maternal or other feeling rather than want. For example, if she had a preschool child she would probably not work. The man would be subject to a support order undoubtedly related to his own needs and plans as well as to his responsibilities. Not only might sounder choices be available all around, but once made they might be held to. The troubled sense of movement to and fro (work-not work, married-separated, in school-out of school) that is characteristic of poor, broken families[168] might be abated.*

---

* Because Americans value personal relations highly, it may be difficult to accept the notion that money can influence relationships in some of the ways described here. It may be useful, therefore, to cite a parallel evaluation of the effects of an *existing* program. The statement is based on a review of five thousand AFDC families in which the quality of child care has been questioned. The reviewers' impression is:

> In many cases, the man is willing to marry the mother of the children, but the mother is unwilling because she needs the security of the ADC check. Although the father sleeps in the home in some cases, he does not marry the mother because he does not earn enough to support the family. The

The significance of stability for the nurture of children is well known. In short, fatherless child insurance might give some families a second try at making the crucial first- and second-stage decisions: when to marry and how to begin work.

FCI would be likely to have substantial impact on poor families as they have more children and experience the full force of the family cycle squeeze. Such insurance might to some extent encourage remarriage. Women living with children are less likely to remarry than those who are childless.[9] There is evidence to suggest that some potential husbands are deterred by the prospect of having to support stepchildren; but if the child were entitled to a benefit of his own continuing to his eighteenth birthday, this problem would be removed.

Apart from this speculative effect, FCI benefits would provide perhaps half of socially orphaned children with a standard of living far from lavish but well above minimum. The figures cited for the average income of orphaned families in Table 7–1 are substantially higher than average survivors' benefits. Apart from benefits, the major source of income for these widowed mothers is earnings—particularly during the years when their children are in school.[210] It may be assumed that the situation would be similar under fatherless child insurance. Social security provides mothers with neutral benefits, subject only to a small reduction if they work. Therefore, FCI beneficiaries with older children would be as likely to work as widowed mothers now are. Those families with a decent benefit and the ability to supplement it would be provided with more than the barest minimum income. It would be late at this point to expect fate to alter the mothers' course but the children, as they approach their own fateful first decisions, would possess the social capital for take-off. They can stay in school, if they choose, until their twenty-second birthday.

mother usually does not expect the father to fully support the children. She counts on some income from him, some ADC, and supplements this income with her earnings.[209]

They lose their benefits if they marry. Not all youngsters would make the choices we desire for them but the opportunities made possible by money lie all in the right direction.

In sum, a program of fatherless child insurance would mitigate or eliminate need for two out of three socially orphaned children (and their mothers). Once initiated, payments would be regular and eminently predictable. To the extent that money can, FCI would provide the leverage for perhaps half of the youths who are socially orphaned to take off toward an adequate income and a stable marriage. Many should use the opportunity.

This summary does not quite dispose of the subject, for we have yet to confront a somewhat different phrasing of the same issues. That is, to the extent that fatherless child insurance offers a payment to children when their parents secure court sanction for a separation, the policy is reminiscent of AFDC. We must, therefore, ask whether the program would encourage family breakdown. We must rearrange our material to provide a direct answer.

In the short run, a number of couples who had been kept together by financial need would probably separate. There should also be a tendency for the separated to secure judicial sanction. These divorces, although they could not be considered a consequence of the program, would show up in higher divorce statistics. As for the long run, a Commissioner's Advisory Committee hazarded the guess that the divorce rate would *decline* as a result of fatherless child insurance.[176] As we have noted, "the tendency to divorce is highest . . . with low occupation and low income." [28] It is reasoned that, if a decent income and living situation can be provided for poor children, they will tend to grow into middle-class or at least somewhat more stable marriage patterns. Further, we have surmised that a certain number of illegitimate relationships might be regularized and more divorced mothers might remarry under FCI. Thus speculation about the net outcome suggests higher divorce and separation rates in the short run and lower rates in the long run. Other aspects of the net outcome are also significant. More parents would find themselves in the marital relationship they preferred. More children would find themselves in a legal family, whether with one parent or two. More children would find themselves with a father.

A CHILD'S PORTION?

The program would involve federal administration of benefits and state and local action on petitions for divorce and separation and administration of fathers' support payments. As a federal program, FCI should be no more difficult to operate than survivors' insurance. Instead of proof of death, proof of divorce or legal separation would be required. A comparatively small number of mothers might receive more from their husbands than from the program. Some would not apply for benefits at all; others might opt out of the program if a court ordered support at a later date.

County or state administration of divorces and legal separations is apt to be more complicated. This would not be the result of fatherless child insurance, except initially when petitions for divorce might be expected to increase, but of the fact that divorce is painful and tedious. It would be very important to help poor people properly through this process, and for this reason special funds would be established to support legal assistance. A substantial amount of money would flow into these funds from fathers under court order. The funds would represent a new, if modest, administrative responsibility in each jurisdiction. Maintaining support orders in appropriate relation to fathers' ability to pay and collecting these sums of money would probably represent a considerable expansion of such current activity.

The impact of FCI on poor children's share of goods and services would not be sharp. To be sure, larger sums of money

125

would go to those poor children who would benefit. Moreover, the formula by which benefits are calculated somewhat favors those who are poorest. On the other hand, benefit payments would also be going to children who would not otherwise have been poor, though proportionately fewer of them; and the financing of the program would fall with equal weight on those who are poor and those who are not. Indeed, intact poor families would make contributions to the program without ever benefiting from it. That social security financing is not more acutely redistributive is, from our point of view, a limitation of this proposal.

ALTERNATIVE LINES OF PROGRAM DEVELOPMENT

The basic concept of applying the insurance principle to socially orphaned children may be developed in various ways. The line of development explored here is the one that seems soundest, on balance. Without undertaking a detailed examination of them, we should at least mention three alternatives.

The requirement of a judicially sanctioned separation limits the number of families reached by the program, and state law or court process may delay a divorce or legal separation for months or even years. In order to extend coverage more quickly and widely, it would be possible to include children whose parents had received a ruling under the Uniform Support of Dependents Law. Under this law, operative in every state, a mother may appear in court to claim lack of support because her husband or the legal father of her child has deserted. The judge makes a finding, which is forwarded to another county or state for support action. Such a finding might establish presumptive entitlement to fatherless child insurance, subject to further proceedings. The process would be more rapid, and coverage would be extended to mothers who could not secure a legal separation. Moreover, the program would achieve a degree of national uniformity that FCI based on state divorce laws must lack. On the other hand, this line of development might subject the program to the problem so familiar in AFDC: a man would be able to provide for his family by deserting them.

The issue of support might also be treated differently. In effect, under the proposal outlined above, the income of mother and children is separated from the father's payment. Thus her husband's support payment, if it failed to come, could be pursued seriously but not out of desperate daily need. On the other hand, this arrangement may destroy the last reason for communication between the father and the mother and children. Particularly if the social insurance payments are inadequate, one may wonder why the mother should be deprived of the support her former husband pays. To meet such objections, the proposed state fund might be abandoned in favor of sending support payments directly to the mother. The amount of the benefit might be adjusted to the support payment on a graduated scale.

Finally, the proposal assumes that FCI, like survivors' insurance, would be financed by a tax on employees and employers. With the enactment of health insurance in 1965, Congress introduced the concept of a government payment as partial support for a program. Because beneficiaries of FCI would be younger, on the average, than survivors and would not have accumulated as much in payments, it could be argued that the government should contribute to the support of the program. From our point of view this would improve the program for it would tend to assure fairer distribution of money among all children. That is, payments would be made in part out of income tax, which is to say, by those who have more. As socially orphaned children tend to be poorer children and as the payment formula favors them, payments would be going in larger part to those who have least.

127

CONCLUSION

In principle, the case for fatherless child insurance is similar to that for survivors' insurance. The prospect of being socially orphaned is, in our society, a major risk to income to which social insurance is the most practical response. In practice, the advantages of fatherless child insurance would be the advantages of social insurance: specificity in reaching a population at risk; benefits that are clear and certain; and a neutral payment that does not interfere with the incentive to work. It would also encourage precisely the family patterns that lead to decent income—a stable family, prolonged education, and reasonably delayed marriage.

The program has several serious disadvantages. Most important, it reaches only a minority of poor children and not all of them adequately. We cannot be satisfied with such a program unless we visualize it in tandem with others that would complete the work. Although FCI might improve the share that poor children receive of the nation's resources, we cannot be certain of this effect. Finally, although we may doubt that it would have such an effect for long or in situations where it would be a misfortune, FCI would be vulnerable to charges of encouraging divorce.

Fatherless child insurance cannot perform the whole task by itself; it might perform a portion of the task very well. Whether it is a necessary element of a national scheme depends on one's evaluation of the alternatives.

8

Negative
Income Tax

✝✝✝✝✝✝✝✝✝✝✝✝✝✝✝✝✝✝✝✝

A second potential program is negative income tax—NEGIT. Three independent principles are usually implied in speaking of NEGIT. First, need is held to be the center of attention, without recourse to euphemism or category. Need is established by a comparatively simple test of income rather than by a means test. In place of an investigatory process and a family-

129

by-family determination of needs and resources, a specified amount of income is declared to be needed. It has been pointed out that, in effect, this process bases payments on "average need." [21] The principle of averaging is not new. The Social Security Administration uses a test of earned income to determine that an aged applicant has retired. The Veterans Administration uses an income test to establish need before paying out certain types of benefits. Second, the name of the proposal implies its source of financing—general revenue funds. Third, the mechanism for administering the program is the income tax return.

Although the negative income tax may have the sound of a new proposal, the idea has cropped up from time to time since the beginning of World War II. Descent is sometimes claimed from the proposal of Lady Juliet Rhys-Williams, in 1942, that the British treat unemployment and disability as risks under social insurance. The only other types of need that would remain, that of dependents (children, wives) and that of the aged, would be met by a regular payment from the national agency responsible for income tax.[153] Lady Rhys-Williams intended a far-reaching redistribution of income and an implicit contract between the individual and the state, the one responsible for production and the other for guaranteeing minimum support. Concretely she intended a flat grant without income test. In her formulation as in Dr. Burns's, a negative income tax is not a guaranteed income. However, she did propose Inland Revenue as the agent for her program.

American proposals fall into three groups, distinguishable rather by their intent than by details. In one group is the proposal of Lewis Meriam, made in 1946, that the tax return substitute for the means test in establishing eligibility for public assistance.[119] Simplicity and a limitation on government expenditure appear to be the purposes here. Milton Friedman made a more or less similar proposal in 1962. He was also interested in simplicity and limited costs and emphasized that his proposal would not interfere with a free economy as, for example, farm subsidies do.[65] A second group includes Senator Hugh Butler's suggestion in 1951 of a basic federal pension of $50 a month, payable—via the income tax return—to all people with incomes under $600 a year. Byron L. Johnson, later to become a Congressman from Colorado, argued that the United States was providing family allowances in the form of income tax deductions and that benefits should be extended downward to those who pay no tax, as a form of family allowance in "the United States framework." [196] The Butler and Johnson proposals intended a modest additional contribution to meeting need. Robert Theobald's proposal is programmatically similar to the others but really represents a third category. Theobald has higher benefit levels in mind and, as we have noted, his objective is to meet a serious new problem of distributing national income.[190]

The negative income tax is more and more frequently mentioned in the United States. Apart from the intensified search for means to achieve social security, broadly understood, specific developments may be responsible for the increased interest. First, the "very success" of social insurance and the income tax has led to the question whether it would not be better to have one rather than two universal, overlapping systems. Second, the increased use of the income tax as a welfare instrument (via special deductions and exemptions) leads to the question whether it might not frankly be used for this purpose.[23] Stanley Surrey, later Assistant Secretary of the Treasury, began pointing almost twenty years ago to the developing use of the income tax as a welfare instrument.[185, 184] His emphasis, however, has been on the irrational nature of the welfare measures that were adopted—barely considered and tending to favor those well off. Finally, the use of tax reductions to stimulate the economy led Lyndon Johnson, among others, to observe that the poor should also directly benefit from tax policy.

Although not widely used abroad, a negative income tax has

131

been in effect in Denmark since 1950. In addition to ordinary income tax deductions for children, for several years families with less than a specified income received a children's allowance. The payment per child varied according to income and rural or urban residence, but no payment was made to families with over 16,000 kroner ($2,319) a year. In recent years, this type of income test has been abandoned; all families receive 400 to 500 kroner ($58 to $72) a year for each child, depending upon the size of the family. The income tax return serves, so to speak, as the application for benefits. Those with sufficient income to be liable for tax receive a credit against it. The others receive a cash payment from their local government which is eventually charged to the national treasury. As the payments are small, this system cannot have a major effect upon need, except in the case of the largest families. However, it extends a benefit from the tax system to those who pay no tax, draws upon the general treasury, and relies for administration upon the income tax return.

It is to be noted that the Danish program is specifically addressed to the needs of children but that various English and American proposals cover all dependents or all needy people. As we are concerned here with the possibilities of a categorical program for children, we shall limit NEGIT as the Danes do. Although the basic principles of a negative income tax are implied by the name, the details of its proposed operation may vary widely. According to one's taste, the content of a proposal may make it appear inconsequential or fantastic. For purposes of discussion, content must nevertheless be provided. We consider the following proposal.

PROPOSAL

Every family with children under eighteen would be expected to file an income tax return. In order to qualify for a NEGIT payment, a husband and wife would have to file a joint return unless they were in fact separated. Any family showing deductions and exemptions in excess of taxable income would receive a cash payment. For purposes of a NEGIT payment, only public assistance payments would be exempted from consideration. (For ordinary tax purposes, social security, unemployment compensation, and similar income are exempted.*) For each $600 of deficit, up to the number of child exemptions in the family, a payment of $300 would be made. The payment would arrive in twelve equal monthly installments following the date on which the return was filed. The cost would be met from general revenues and, it has been noted, would appear in the federal budget as a net reduction in tax collections.[102]

The intention of these specifications can be readily stated. The payment of $25 a month per needy child is large enough to have some effect on need. (AFDC payments, for example, average $34 per person a month.) Further along we shall come to the reasons why a higher payment has not been proposed. The payment is not calculated on a progressive scale analogous to income tax payments. Although such a scale has a superficial appeal to equity, payments in the lower percentages would be trivial amounts. A scale would also be more complicated to administer and understand. In principle, even the $25 payment may make an appeal to the concept of equity. Those below the poverty line are in effect paid benefits at a 50 per cent rate, like the well-to-do who pay a tax at the rate of 50 per cent.

If husbands and wives were permitted the regular option to file separately, every mother without income of her own might qualify for a $25-a-month payment, while her husband paid only the tax that a $600 exemption per dependent was worth to him— as little as $7 a month. Spacing payments over a year is intended to avoid putting large lump sums into the hands of people unac-

---

* Some would find themselves not liable for tax and yet, when social security or other exempt income is taken into account, not entitled to NEGIT payment— fair enough!

customed to dealing with them. The mechanism of the income tax return seems to imply after-the-fact payment rather than payment from the first moment a family feels they are in need. A child born any time during the prior year would constitute an exemption, however, so that the delay in benefits would be considerably less than a year for many. It would, of course, be possible to establish a system of Declarations of Estimated Deficit, but again we choose to avoid a large complication.

It has been pointed out that exempt income could, in a program of NEGIT, lead to substantial inequity.[79] It does not make sense, for example, that NEGIT might be paid concurrently with decent social security or unemployment compensation. For this reason, such payments are counted like other income. As for public assistance, NEGIT should be regarded as the basic program and public assistance as the second line of defense. To achieve this, public assistance would be exempt for purposes of negative income tax as it is for income tax. Once a family's entitlement to NEGIT was established, their public assistance payments would routinely be adjusted.

In order to evaluate the proposal, we turn now to its coverage and impact, its effect on the family-income cycle and on incentive, and certain broader effects. We shall, with the exceptions already stated, treat the income tax as an established structure for the program. However, it should be borne in mind that the tax law is itself subject to change.

COVERAGE AND IMPACT

Roughly speaking, the point at which a family shows a deficit for income tax purposes approximates the budget amounts we are using as the brink of poverty. Table 8–1 will make this clear. In families of two to four members (as many as two children in intact families, up to three children in broken families) the pro-

TABLE 8-1.   *Comparison of Income Tax and Poverty Index*

SIZE OF FAMILY	VALUE OF EXEMPTIONS AND MINIMUM STANDARD DEDUCTION IN INCOME TAX	POVERTY INDEX OF THE SOCIAL SECURITY ADMINISTRATION (NON-FARM FAMILIES)
2 members	$1,600	$1,990
3 members	2,300	2,440
4 members	3,000	3,130
5 members	3,700	3,685
6 members	4,400	4,135
7 members	5,100	4,600

Source: The income tax column is based on the sum of one exemption for each member of the family and the minimum standard deduction for the family. Development of the Poverty Index is explained in Mollie Orshansky, "Counting the Poor: Another Look at the Poverty Profile," *Social Security Bulletin*, Vol. 28, No. 1 (January 1965).[138]

gram would not come into play until a bit below the level of poverty. Among larger families, the program would be in effect at and a bit above the level defined as poverty.

If we apply the income tax levels in Table 8-1 to data about family income in 1963, it develops that the program defined would make payments for 11.6 million children in 4.5 million poor families, but no payments would be made for 3.4 million poor children. About a quarter of a million poor though small families with children would receive no payments at all. Perhaps half a million larger families would receive a payment for one child, though their income before benefits would be a bit over the poverty level. The gross cost, ignoring possible savings such as in public assistance, would be $3.5 billion.

These estimates of coverage and cost must be regarded as conservative. For reasons inherent in the data, it is not possible either to allow deductions for people in a household other than parents and children or to exclude their income from family income. Indications are that a substantial percentage of smaller

135

families include such relatives or friends. Also, the estimate deals only with minimum standard deductions; some families would obviously have larger permissible deductions (medical care, child care). We conclude that 80 per cent or more of poor children would receive some payment under NEGIT. Virtually all poor families and a few not quite poor would be reached with payments for at least one child.

Coverage cannot be considered apart from impact. Rather than generalize, Table 8–2 selects three representative types of family and describes the impact NEGIT would have at each income level. These examples merely illustrate what we might plausibly have inferred from the definition of the program and the accidental relationship of income tax provisions and the poverty budget. A few families receive enough money so as no longer to be defined as poor. (For example, a family of four with $2,900 receives $300.) On the average, however, families receive about half the difference between what they have and what, at an absolute minimum, they need. We noted earlier that families with children have, in total, three fifths of the income they need. With a program of NEGIT, as defined here, they would have a bit over four fifths of the income they need. Because the program is written for children* and because income tax provisions give larger families an edge in relation to the definition of poverty, the negative income tax payment would meet a greater proportion of the deficit of larger families than of smaller families.

The discussion so far is based on the assumption that the negative income tax payment would represent additional income for all families. Conceivably, however, the entry of NEGIT would spell the exit or diminution of AFDC. In 1963 about one out of

---

* Families with enough children to receive payments based on their whole deficit receive, on the average, well over 50 per cent of the deficit. A family with a deficit of $1,000 and two children receives $600 in payment, for example. On the other hand, families with fewer children in relation to their income deficit receive well under 50 per cent. A family with a deficit of $1,000 and one child receives $300 in payments.

TABLE 8–2. *Impact of a Program of Negative Income Tax on Selected Families, 1963*

Husband-Wife Family with Two Children	Female-Headed Family with Three Children	Husband-Wife Family with Five Children
210,000 families with income of $2,400–$3,000 receive $300 a year	40,000 families with income of $2,400–$3,000 receive $300 a year	14,000 families with income of $4,500–$5,100 receive $300 a year
357,000 families with income under $2,400 receive $600 a year	64,000 families with income of $1,800–$2,400 receive $600 a year	76,000 families with income of $3,900–$4,500 receive $600 a year
	227,000 families with income under $1,800 receive $900 a year	67,000 families with income of $3,300–$3,900 receive $900 a year
		75,000 families with income of $2,700–$3,300 receive $1,200 a year
		154,000 families with income under $2,700 receive $1,500 a year
Total: 567,000 families—payment for 924,000 children	Total: 331,000 families—payment for 849,000 children	Total: 386,000 families—payment for 1,437,000 children
Poverty level—$3,130	Poverty level—$3,115	Poverty level—$4,600
Median[a] income of all families before NEGIT—$2,220	Median[a] income of all families before NEGIT—$1,490	Median[a] income of all families before NEGIT—$3,320
Mean[a] additional income provided per family by NEGIT—$490	Mean[a] additional income provided per family by NEGIT—$770	Mean[a] additional income provided per family by NEGIT—$1,120

Note: Detailed data are provided in Appendix II.

[a] The mean cannot be added to the median to produce a new average. Families below the median are receiving a larger increase than people above it.

four poor children benefited from AFDC.[138] Thus it could be argued that estimates of coverage or impact ought to be reduced in order to allow for withdrawal of AFDC. We stipulate that in accordance with our earlier observations about the means test, a shift from AFDC to NEGIT would itself be desirable. Yet that gain is not sufficient if it means continuing to fall short of the objective of providing sufficient goods to children.* The alternative would be that NEGIT should not replace AFDC. Budget standards, inadequate almost everywhere, might be raised and eligibility requirements liberalized. The future in this is hard to determine, and one takes his choice. For our purposes we shall assume every effort would be made to induce welfare departments to reinvest any money that might be saved in such a way as to assure children a standard of living above the poverty level. As our figures indicate, NEGIT would leave much room for such activity.

THE FAMILY-INCOME CYCLE

NEGIT might be expected to come into play very early in the family cycle—within a few months of the birth of the first child. It would provide income for a child living with both his parents as well as for the child alone with his mother. The amount of income, however, could hardly be expected to influence the occupational choice of the young husband. Torn between school and work or between taking the first job he sees and waiting for a promising one, he would not be helped much by the assurance of $25 a month.

NEGIT should have more meaning later on in marriage,

---

* For example, a mother with three children earns $1,900 a year and receives $50 a month AFDC. If a NEGIT payment of $600 a year means she will no longer receive AFDC, she is just as far from the poverty level as ever.

when the family cycle squeeze is really being felt. At that time families with substantial deficits and three or four children or more could count on income in excess of $100 a month. Such assurance (combined with any savings or help from other members of the family) might encourage some men to move if work is more readily available in another area. (Public assistance may be available at home, but it is generally unavailable in another state.) A different effect of government support might be to encourage some men to resign from work that brought substandard pay in order to seek better work or job training. NEGIT would at least establish a floor for income, inadequate though it would be, and a substantial supplement to other resources (family help, savings) if they exist. However, we have said that it is late to expect change at this stage. For the majority of beneficiaries experiencing family cycle squeeze, the assurance of income would represent a substantial easing of their plight. As Table 8–2 and Appendix II show, they would receive cash payments representing several multiples of $300 a year. But it is in the nature of the program that they would still have a substantial deficit.

For the young teenager growing up in a family receiving NEGIT to know that the government is contributing $25 a month toward his support may conceivably justify his postponing the hardships of adulthood. If he is so moved, his family may continue to receive this amount of money while he pursues his education further. In fact, income tax and NEGIT provisions combine to make payment possible beyond eighteen years if he does continue in school. This might occur in comparatively few families. There are other minor ways in which NEGIT might alter family fates. The $300 that families with a very nearly minimum income receive might give them a bit of flexibility. The fact that payment would be made after need had been established would mean that a few families already on the way up would have an added several hundred dollars to assist them.

Finally, the negative income tax would be simple to understand and virtually automatic in operation. It would be, as we have said it should be, predictable and where necessary continuous. It would thus simplify management and planning for poor people and, to the extent that administrative process can, support their efforts to improve their circumstances.

Apart from income development, NEGIT might be expected also to have minor constructive effects on family stability. In poor families the advent of a child would bring a small increment in family income (even if not enough to support it), which might moderate the impulse of some fathers to flee. We observed that a program of fatherless child insurance might encourage a certain number of remarriages. Obviously NEGIT is not the type of incentive matchmakers offer, but where there is an inclination to marry it too may help to decide the matter. Finally, we have observed that some children are separated from their families for financial reasons. To the degree that NEGIT provides sufficient income to avoid this, it would assure a child an upbringing by his own family.

We perceive that NEGIT would substantially but not adequately ameliorate the situation of poor families. With the exception of families in marginal situations, it could not be regarded as a powerful lever to turn them in a new direction. The program lacks power mainly because payments are small, which raises the question whether its influence might be enhanced by increasing payments. Unfortunately increased payments create a problem in relation to the incentive to work.

As formulated NEGIT would not alter a man's drive to work or even discourage a mother with young children from working. NEGIT provides roughly half of what men and women might earn themselves in income brackets in which the other half would be desperately needed. Moreover, additional income would not affect a NEGIT payment until the following year. It would require a degree of foresight that poor people supposedly do not possess

140

to avoid work now in order to receive half as much money next year.*

Difficulties arise when one moves beyond payments that approximate 50 per cent of the deficit. Meaningful sums of money would be made available to people with marginal incomes. For example, paying 75 instead of 50 per cent of the deficit would lead to the following situations: A couple with two children and earned income of $1,800 receives NEGIT of $900. For every $4 they earn as their earned income rises from $1,800 to $3,000, they lose $3. A mother with five children and insurance benefits of $2,600 receives NEGIT of $1,800. For every $4 she earns as her own income rises from $2,600 to $4,400, she loses $3. Prospective loss of this magnitude is too large to ignore. As we concluded in Chapter 4, tying benefits to income produces a problem for people whose income cannot greatly exceed payments.

If payments were larger, a parallel problem would also arise in relation to a man's presence in the home with his wife and children. The exemption for each child is worth $84 a year to a man with comparatively small income. The difference between that and a $300 NEGIT payment is consequential but hardly enough to make it worthwhile for him to establish a separate household, speaking in financial terms alone. If the payment rises substantially, however, NEGIT would indeed face the problem that has been laid at the door of AFDC—that a man with a small income could increase the income of his family by leaving it. Apart from whether men did in fact leave their families, the temptation to report separation would be strong and the govern-

---

* Actually, under the proposal, a family that failed by just a few dollars to show a deficit for the preceding year might lose a $300 payment. However, having earned a bit more than the break-even amount in the preceding year, a family might reasonably hope to increase its earnings in the current year by $300 or even more. Thus the route to higher income remains open. This problem can be avoided entirely by paying exactly 50 per cent of the deficit each year, rather than multiples of $300. We favor the multiples because they are simpler to understand and budget and they amount, on the average, to larger payments.

ment would be involved in a knotty problem of how decently to define and determine whether a man and woman are living together.

Thus the NEGIT payments we may consider are kept small by two factors: First, NEGIT operates within the limits of allowable exemptions and deductions under income tax law. Though these are adapted to our purposes, we begin and end with modest sums of money. Second is the incentive problem, in relation to incentive to work and also in relation to incentive to maintain an intact home. With substantial payments the problem looms large. It is possible to make more substantial payments, even within the limitation of paying 50 per cent of the deficit, by altering the figures established by the income tax and expanding our view of what families might be included. This possibility will be outlined as an alternative line of program development.

DIVIDING NATIONAL INCOME

Because eligibility for negative income tax is based on simple conditions, it ought to be comparatively inexpensive to administer. Only 8 per cent of the population is not somehow accounted for in current income tax returns; the addition to the total volume of returns under NEGIT would be small. Control would be exercised by auditing sample returns, as is the current practice. It is difficult to conceive of a simpler means of administering a program in which any connection is to be retained between personal income and benefits.

We have said that one objective of an income maintenance program is to provide the families in which poor children are now living with a fairer share of the national income. In 1963 the total income of families with poor children was about $10 billion, if public assistance and other transfer payments are included.[138] NEGIT would add $3.5 billion to their income. Their eligibility for benefits would increase with prices—as deductible items increase in cost and as Congress chooses to alter the value of exemptions. Without going into the subsequent effects of such an increase on prices and production, we can say that NEGIT would amount to an immediate increase in income of about a third. This is a net gain, as no income increases are contemplated for families that are not poor.

Finally, we observe that without a means test NEGIT builds a new program on the distinction between those who have and those who have not enough money. Making this distinction provides the maximum opportunity for funneling money precisely to people who need it. But those who benefit are thereby identified as poor. We cannot predict whether by being so identified poor people would become the target in the 1970's, as they were in the 1950's, of widespread criticism concerning their life patterns, honesty, and morality. If this happened, it would not only be unfortunate in itself but would probably result in legislative limitation on the amounts of money devoted to NEGIT.

ALTERNATIVE LINES OF PROGRAM DEVELOPMENT

The proposed form of NEGIT is constrained by current provisions of the income tax law. It makes payments in accordance with the deductions and exemptions allowable under the law for other purposes. This fact, taken together with the limitation on the percentage of the deficit that can be met, results in rather small payments. This limitation may be avoided in some measure by replacing current provisions with a larger exemption; and in the course of making such a change the calculation can be greatly simplified, an incidental but significant gain.

James Tobin has offered such a plan.[193] In effect the plan establishes a base of $1,200 per person in a family. After a fam-

143

ily's income is taken into account, a government payment would meet one third of the remaining deficit. (Other specifications of the proposal may be found in Professor Tobin's summary statement, Appendix IV.) Although families with no other income would still be in difficulty, families with some earning ability would find this form of NEGIT a powerful aid. For example, a family of six with an income of $4,000 would receive a government payment of over $1,000. Instead of being poor, they would have some margin above poverty.

The proposal is expensive—involving about $15 billion—and is broader than a program for children. It is an illustration, however, of the possibility of using NEGIT as a means of distributing substantial amounts of money, provided there is a willingness to alter the income tax structure.

We should note that, with further alteration of the income tax structure, one arrives readily at a plan that would afford a guaranteed income, in the strictest sense of the term. Instead of paying $400 each to people with no other income, the government might pay $400 to everyone in the country. At the same time, exemptions and deductions might be eliminated from the income tax; tax rates would doubtlessly have to be restructured to recapture part of the cost from those with the highest incomes. Analysis of such a plan is not within our purview. We simply note that, although it may sound similar to the Tobin proposal, it in fact involves a payment to everyone in the country, without an income test—it is, in other words, a guaranteed minimum income.

CONCLUSION

The negative income tax offers a simple, easily administered mechanism for mitigating the needs of poor children. Because it incorporates an income test, it requires careful evaluation as to its effect on the incentive to work or to secure other income. With modest benefits the problem would not be serious. On the other hand, the provision of modest benefits would bring children only slightly more than halfway toward acquiring the barest minimum of the goods and services they need.

Meeting need, to the degree that it brings about better nutrition, housing, and medical care, helps families take a step toward securing an adequate income. Beyond this, NEGIT is not a powerful instrument for take-off. It provides a very few families with a very small surplus. It does not intervene with special force at the points we have called critical—when the family sets out as a family and when teenagers begin to make choices of their own. Apart from the explicit objectives of the program, one can visuaulize constructive effects in that a small number of families would be held intact by the program. No actually destructive family effects seem likely. The negative income tax would tend to give poor children a fairer share of the national income than they now have. The net distribution of goods and services would, of course, be determined by many other choices as well.

In short, the negative income tax provides a simple instrument for broad-scale alleviation of children's needs. Would it lead many families to take-off; would it give many children power over their futures? Hardly. The nation might do worse. Whether it might do better depends on one's evaluation of alternative programs.

Family
Allowances

✝✝✝✝✝✝✝✝✝✝✝✝✝✝✝✝✝✝✝✝

Of the two family characteristics that
lead to childhood poverty but are in no way relieved by social
insurance, fatherless child insurance would deal with one. The
other family characteristic that makes children vulnerable to
poverty is size. If one selects at random a family with six or more

children, the chances are even that they are poor. To put it another way, three out of five poor children are members of families with four or more children. The problem for children is not simply that more children require more family income. Life is harder than that, for larger families have not the same incomes as small families but even lower incomes. In 1963 families consisting of a mother and two children had a median income of $2,910 but mothers with five children had $1,660. Similarly, married couples with two children had $7,180, but couples with five children had $6,380.[139] We have dwelt on the double trouble at the heart of these figures: large families may mean not only higher costs but a competitive disadvantage in improving income. One means of avoiding this disadvantage while doing something for all children is a program of family allowances.

Family allowances may be defined as regular payments for children made without regard to family income or other eligibility conditions. The definition thus does not include public assistance or survivors' insurance. In the operation of these programs, payments may be adjusted to the number of children but a major criterion other than childhood (need, loss of a parent) is involved. The term "family allowance" is occasionally used to include programs that operate within the limits of an income test. Such programs more or less resemble a negative income tax; but, as we have already considered the negative income tax, we shall omit this meaning from the definition of family allowance used here.

The concept of family allowances has antecedents that reach back nearly two hundred years. The British "Speenhamland system," though it is suggestive of the negative income tax, is usually regarded as an ancestor of family allowances. Opposing a minimum wage in 1796, the Prime Minister offered to "make relief, in cases where there are a number of children, a matter of right and an honor instead of a ground for opprobrium and contempt." [216] There followed a short-lived experiment in subsidizing incomes up to varying amounts, depending on the number of children in the family.

On the continent at the end of the nineteenth century, a number of French firms were adjusting wages to employees' family size. This practice spread widely after World War I—clearly as a strategy for meeting family needs without raising wages generally. After World War II family allowances expanded more widely, by this time under government auspices. A majority of the countries of the world and all of the industrialized West, except the United States, now have such programs. The postwar expansion of family allowances represented a new sense of national responsibility for children and for the avoidance of want. In Europe the wish to raise the birth rate was at least a subsidiary motive. The wish to place a ceiling on wages was now either absent[11] or, as in France, explicitly rejected.[170]

Neighboring Canada has a twenty-year-old program of family allowances. An allowance is paid for all children who are under sixteen and in school. For children under ten, the benefit is $6 a month; for older children, $8. The benefit is normally paid to the mother. The national government bears the total cost. To find a program with substantial payments one must look to France. The payment there varies according to region, the number of children in a family, and their ages. In Paris in 1964, for example, a family with four children received between 380 and 545 francs ($77 to $111) a month, exceeding the legal minimum wage at that time. In addition, various special payments may be made: during pregnancy, at birth, for improved housing. Eligibility depends upon a parent's employment, but exceptions are made and coverage is thought to be virtually universal. The cost is met by a tax on wages paid by employers only. In 1964 the tax rate was 13.5 per cent of wages up to $2,130 a year.

In the United States interest in family allowances has been sporadic. In the mid-1920's Senator Paul Douglas put forward a proposal with which he had taken some pains, attempting to resolve "this dilemma in which our whole wage policy finds itself." [43] The dilemma lay in trying to set a minimum wage that would meet the needs of large families without unduly burdening the economy. The way out appeared to lie in fixing a minimum wage for single men that would be supplemented by allowances for dependents. During the depression there were scattered discussions of family allowances.[51] Following World War II, apparently in response to developments in other countries, several proposals and analyses appeared.[26, 38, 216] In 1955 a number of prominent Senators proposed a study that might have led to the enactment of a program, but the Senate did not pass the resolution.*

There are probably two major reasons why sentiment in the United States has remained cool to the idea of family allowances. In their statement on the proposed Senate resolution, the Executive Council of the AFL-CIO gave one reason.

Family allowances [the AFL-CIO said] would represent a considerable departure from the traditional American concept of the living wage. Labor in this country has preferred other approaches to the same objective, through such methods as tax exemptions for dependents, minimum wages, public assistance, social security, etc.[4]

The Executive Council nevertheless recognized that many children were needy and recommended further study of family allowances. The other major reason why family allowances have not received substantial consideration may lie in public attitudes about the national birth rate and religion. As we have noted, interest in raising the birth rate has been a prominent reason why some countries have enacted programs. Americans have not typically been eager to increase the overall birth rate. It has widely been assumed that family allowances would be a Catholic meas-

* S. Resolution 109, submitted June 14, 1955, by Senators Neuberger, Morse, Douglas, Humphrey, Kefauver, Lehman, Kennedy, and McNamara.

ure; and the relationship of church and government being what it is in twentieth-century America, it has been difficult to enact any national measure that became defined as sectarian.

Although no program of family allowances has ever neared adoption in this country, the principle that income should be adjusted to number of children has been incorporated in a variety of government activities. The income tax offers credit worth upwards of $84 per child (that is, a $600 exemption at a minimum tax rate of 14 per cent) to families with sufficient income to profit from it. During the war the government paid a serviceman's family monthly, in addition to his own contribution, $40 for his wife and one child and $10 for each additional child. The rationale— explicitly rejected by Congress in setting peacetime compensation —was to assist in the support of larger families. In the development of the social security system, benefits have been related to the number of dependents in a family. In administering workmen's compensation and unemployment insurance, a minority of the states provide allowances for dependents in addition to the basic benefit. Some public school systems have paid teachers in accordance with their family responsibilities. The practice persists in a few small school districts, despite formal opposition from the National Education Association.

NONPROPOSAL

A straightforward proposal for family allowances (which we will state only to abandon) might be made as follows: For the first child in a family, while he is under eighteen and in school, an allowance of $10 a month would be paid. For all subsequent children the benefit would be $40 a month. The cost would be borne out of general revenue. The present income tax exemption for children would be eliminated and the allowance would be taxable. Family benefits in social security would be adjusted downward and in other programs eliminated.

150

The amount of $40 is selected because it slightly exceeds the average per child expenditure in AFDC. It would at least affect childhood poverty to the degree that AFDC now does. The benefit for the first child is nominal, so as to help limit the cost of the program and to concentrate on relieving family cycle squeeze. As families would receive directly the value of exemptions for children, those exemptions for tax purposes would be eliminated. For similar reasons, social security and other programs would not need to provide as high benefits for dependents as they do now. The changes in the tax and social security structures would assist in reducing the net cost of the family allowance program.

Even so, the net cost would amount to about $14 billion, allowing for savings in taxes, social security, and public assistance. We have noted that the aggregate deficit of all poor families in the United States, including those without children, is only $11 to $12 billion. Furthermore, calculations make clear that the payment envisioned would not eradicate poverty even among children. For example, of poor families with three children (families large enough to benefit), fewer than half would be brought over the poverty level. For an amount of money greater than the combined deficit all poor people suffer, we expect a larger return. It does not therefore seem reasonable to analyze this straightforward proposal in further detail. Instead we present for consideration a more modest proposal for family allowances.

A MODEST PROPOSAL

A benefit of $50 a month would be payable for each child under six years of age. The cost would be borne out of general revenue. Present income tax exemptions for all children would be eliminated, and the benefit itself would be taxable. To distinguish this

151

proposal from one of family allowances for all children up to eighteen years of age, we shall call it a preschool allowance.

A preschool allowance provides more money for each eligible child but reduces the total cost through several devices. First, the program concentrates on one of the two periods we have called crucial. Second, the benefit is itself taxable. Although it may seem unjust that the poorest families may have to pay taxes, they will be paying at the lowest rate. A tax-free allowance would support a lower level of benefits; poor families would lose more in accepting a lower level of benefits than by paying taxes on somewhat higher benefits. Third, the overall cost is reduced by wiping out the income tax exemption for all children, regardless of age. Families with an adequate income would not lose money in the long run, a point to which we will return.

We do not without concern preclude children six and over from the benefits of the proposal. In doing so, we will fail to deal with the poverty of many children and we will not deal with it effectively in the case of the large families who are usually regarded as the major beneficiaries of family allowances. Two steps should be taken on behalf of the children left out. First, money released to public assistance by preschool allowances should be redirected to assuring older children more nearly adequate assistance. (In calculating the cost of preschool allowances, therefore, we will not estimate net savings in public assistance.)

Second, we have noted that assistance given in the form of public services is tending to be directed through the schools. Health services, diet supplements, vocational aids, and cultural opportunities are almost naturally distributed in connection with school. Moreover, the concentration of public services where geographically they appear to be needed may avoid the cost of universal service programs without creating the potential problems of an income test (onus and incentive). We assume, therefore, that a program of preschool allowances would be accompanied by a vastly expanded program of public services for children who are in school. Not all these services need actually be administered by schools. Like recreation services, they may also be administered by other agencies for children old enough to take advantage of them. With the passage of the Economic Opportunity Act and the 1965 Education Act the nation has already moved toward expanded public services.

REACH OF THE PROPOSAL

The program described would reach all children below the age of six and, as we shall see, some older children. It would cost $5.9 billion a year.*

The data required to calculate the impact of such a program accurately—classifying income simultaneously by size of family and age of children—are not available. We do know that, of poor families with children, almost two thirds have children under six and they average two preschool children per family. In 1964 these families had an average income of $2,307.[147] The preschool allowance would raise their average income to about $3,300, which is about $14 a month above the poverty level for a family of four. A substantial minority of these families were families of three. Rather more of them included older children and other family members and were therefore families of five, six, or more. In other words, half or perhaps somewhat fewer families with children under six would be brought out of poverty by a program of preschool allowances. For the rest, poverty would be substantially ameliorated.

We may approach the question of impact differently by rea-

* In 1964 there were 24,836,000 children under six in the United States. At $600 for each, the gross cost would amount to $14.9 billion. Tax collected on this income may be estimated at $2 billion and collections resulting from wiping out the income tax exemption for all children may be estimated at $7 billion. Of the gross cost of $14.9 billion, $9 billion would be recaptured—leaving a net cost of $5.9 billion.

soning from the effect of a $600 payment for *all* children in the country. Of 15.6 million children in 4.7 million poor families, four million children in 1.8 million families would remain poor.* About three out of four of the children who concern us would find themselves in families no longer poor. Of the 4 million children who remained poor, the majority would have received three fourths or more of their deficit. Though still poor, they would have been brought within hailing distance of the line. Obviously a program of payments to all children exaggerates the impact of a preschool program on preschool children—apparently by about 50 per cent. However, we may assume that these proportions would apply to the first years of family life, when all children in a particular family are under six. Of ten poor families in this first stage, we may thus anticipate that the program defined would avert poverty for seven or eight, and come close to averting it for one. One family out of ten in the first stage would not even come close to escaping poverty.

After several years the impact on each family would begin to decline. As each child reached school age, the family allowance would be reduced and the family might conceivably be poor as a result. As income is pooled for family spending, younger children would probably suffer as well as older children, even though they were still receiving an allowance. The corollary of this statement is that older children in poor families would benefit from the program as long as they had younger brothers and sisters.

* Allowing for the lowest tax rate (14 per cent) on the $600 allowance, the net value of the allowance to poor families is calculated at $514. Since this assumption exaggerates the total tax that poor families would pay, the initial calculation (4,324,000 children in 1,906,000 families) is rounded down.

The data on which this estimate is based [139] show the current income of poor families, including public assistance. The estimate would be accurate only if public assistance were not reduced as a consequence of the allowance payments. This effect could be achieved by exempting the allowance from consideration as income for purposes of public assistance or by raising public assistance standards.

The impact of a family allowance program has been described so far in terms of whether families would be freed from poverty. We have said, however, that optimum conditions for take-off include some surplus of income over the barest minimum needs. In order to estimate how well the proposal would achieve a surplus, we must again make an inference from data dealing with all poor children. (Details of the data used are provided in the first table in Appendix III.) The major effect would be felt during the first six years in which a family received an allowance. In these years, half the children we have said would not be poor might find themselves in families with at least $650 over the poverty level we have defined. The greatest impact would be felt in the largest families. After the initial six years, the program would tend less and less to provide a surplus.

In sum, the proposed program of allowances would reach all preschool children. Those in young families would be reached with substantial effectiveness. The effectiveness of the program in averting poverty would decline as one child after another in a family reached school age.

BUT WOULD IT ALTER FATE?

In that the payment is assured and substantial, the effects of preschool allowances would resemble the effects of fatherless child insurance. The two proposals differ in that one selects for aid all young children and the other children of any age who are socially orphaned. In cases of premarital pregnancy preschool allowances would exert a more neutral influence than FCI. Though FCI would provide an incentive for marriage, the family allowance would be available for the child whether or not his parents were married. The preschool allowance provides no incentive for marriage; in fact it assures an income to illegitimate children—who may need it most.

155

In any event, the large majority of families begin with marriage. Once a family was started, the preschool allowance would provide a poverty-free period of at least six years for most. Half of the children who would otherwise have been poor would find themselves in families with a substantial surplus of income over minimum requirements—substantial in any terms they might have known. As we have seen, the beginning of the family is the crucial period in which family and vocational patterns are established. Under a program of preschool allowances a family would have an income it could depend on at this critical time. It would be able to plan a move, a job change, or training with comparative certainty about its resources. The arrival of a child should not be an immediate financial blow for a family, one that precipitates the father to flight or abandonment of plans for self-advancement. Food, shelter, and clothing should be adequate, providing biological permission for optimism, pride, and ambition.

As their first children reached school age, families would experience the family cycle squeeze—but with modified force. Mothers and fathers would be in their mid-twenties or older, and family income would have advanced beyond its initial low point. Moreover, the family would be losing the preschool allowance in stages. The mother presumably would have chosen to stay home while her children were of preschool age. The children's entrance into school would provide her with the incentive and opportunity to work. Her income would help take up the deficit left by the termination of the preschool allowance.* Finally, school-centered programs and somewhat more adequate public assistance might meet the continuing needs of older children.

Preschool allowances might be expected to help promote intact families. For one thing, mothers would be encouraged to

---

* ". . . the proportions of all families found in poverty diminishes as age removes the hindrance of such children [under six] to increased family earnings . . ." [147]

remarry. Children for whom there was some financial provision would be somewhat less likely to be regarded as financial liabilities by potential stepfathers. On the other hand, probably some married couples stay together only because their income is insufficient to support separate households. Some small number of such marriages might dissolve with increased income; whether such dissolutions would be regrettable is another question. But these are short-range effects. In the long run, decent income might be expected to lead to more nearly middle-class views of marriage and therefore greater stability.

The proposal does not have any direct bearing on the second crucial period of a poor family's development—when children in their young teens are formulating the choices that will set their own family and income patterns. In terms of the family-income cycle, this is the major limitation of the proposal: it spends all its force on children in the preschool years. The early impact should be substantial, but if the program fails to achieve its objectives, a family may experience chronic low income during the time when their children are in school. In that event, the program does not have any renewed effect until a new family has started.

Just as one inevitably is led to wonder whether fatherless child insurance would encourage family breakdown, it seems natural to ask whether preschool allowances would encourage a higher birth rate. We have already dealt with this issue in some detail. It might be anticipated that some poor families would go ahead and have more children because preschool allowances held out a means of supporting them. (Such families must, of course, expect to assume support after the children are six years old.) But the weight of evidence is that large poor families result from an inability to control family size rather than from an express wish. It must be supposed that at least as many couples would find in decent income the resources and reason for limiting their families as for having more children. We have concluded that the net birth rate is more likely to respond to other forces (economic conditions, style) than to a new income maintenance program. In the long run, if people are indeed helped to move up, their child-bearing patterns might be expected to converge with those of other middle-class families—that is, they would have no more than three or four children.

THOSE WHO ARE NOT POOR

General improvement of the quality of child care, whether or not children are poor, is not our objective here. Yet three fourths of the children who would be reached by a new income maintenance program are not poor. If the effects of the program on them were merely neutral, then that money would be wasted. Children who are not poor obviously do not need such a program to the extent that poor children do; yet it may be anticipated that they would benefit to some degree. The early child-bearing years put pressure on middle-income families as well as poor ones. Their income is then at its lowest, and they are making the sacrifices in the interests of self-advancement that we wish poor people to make.

There is, in fact, evidence that large families with incomes a good deal higher than the poverty level suffer compared with smaller families. A series of English studies establish that larger families *in every income bracket* have a higher rate of infant mortality, poor nutrition, and poor educational attainment.[113] No American studies are available either to confirm or to contradict this finding, but is it reasonable to assume that middle-class families in the United States fare better than high-income families in England? Large families with adequate incomes may have a special family pattern; infant mortality in large families may indeed have biological causes. However, as Tony Lynes writes:

. . . the crucial question is not whether the handicaps of the child in a large family are caused solely by the inadequacy of the family income, but rather whether an increase in the family income can help to counteract these handicaps.[113]

Those who have a satisfactory income—and several children—would benefit by a program of preschool allowances as well as poor families. Such a program would in effect bring forward a portion of their decent life incomes to the time when their income was least adequate to their needs. The quality of care for middle-income children should therefore improve.

FAIR SHARES?

We should be more exact about the effects of preschool allowances on the distribution of income. A family that pays a tax of 25 per cent on its highest income (net taxable income of about $12,000) would find that the preschool allowance provided as much income in six years as would otherwise have been saved in taxes in eighteen years. That is, of each $600 a year the family received in allowances, it would retain $450—for six years. Under 1966 tax laws, the same family would save $150 a year in taxes for eighteen years.* Families with higher incomes would register a net loss under the proposal compared with what they would otherwise receive for a child. Families with taxable incomes of $4,000 to $10,000 would register a small net gain for each child, as extra income would be taxed at a rate of about 20 per cent. Poor families should show the largest gain, $514 a year or more for each

---

* Actually few families have a stable income for eighteen years; most start with a lower income and slowly acquire a higher income. Families that rise from a lower income to a net taxable income of $12,000 after several years of marriage would, under the proposal, register a small net gain compared with their experience under 1966 tax laws.

child. Thus, in the framework of the income tax provisions for children, the effect of preschool allowances would be: (1) to bring the benefit forward to an earlier point in the family cycle, and (2) to reapportion the current federal subsidy in order to favor poor children. These two reallocations would account for more than half the money actually paid out. The remaining $5.9 billion, representing the net cost of the program, would come from general revenue. That portion of the cost would be borne rather more by those with middle and higher incomes than by low-income families.

It is implicit in what has already been said that the problem of incentive to work does not arise under a program of preschool allowances; the program permits families to do, without penalty, what they consider to be to their benefit. Nor would any group be stigmatized for receiving support. Young children would receive allowances as older children receive free schooling—as a matter of right.

As family allowances were, in origin at least, intended as a device to limit wages, we should take note of this issue. A program of preschool allowances might affect wage levels in two ways, through influencing the number of people available for work and through the collective bargaining process. With a program of preschool allowances the make-up of the labor force might change in the following ways. In 1960, 2.4 million women with children under six were working;[197] if those women had an assured income, the number of them in the working force might somewhat decline. As the problem of incentive does not arise, the number of men at work would be unaffected. The program indirectly ameliorates the situation of some older children who are poor; conceivably a few of them would delay beginning work. In sum, the effect of the program on the number who want to work would not be large. The demand for goods would be unaffected—not to say higher—and the labor force, if affected at all, somewhat

160

smaller. If salaries and wages responded at all to these conditions, they could only rise.

Earlier it was thought that a program of family allowances would weaken the position of the worker or trade union in collective bargaining. An employer might take the position that allowances meet the needs of the employees' children; therefore salaries need meet only the needs of adults. However, collective bargaining has not for many years been conducted in the United States in order to secure a "living wage." At issue, rather, has been what increases are necessary in order to meet rising costs and to provide employees with a share of rising productivity. The determination of neither issue would be greatly altered by a program of allowances. Apart from costs and productivity, the results of collective bargaining are also affected by economic conditions which may for the moment strengthen employers or employees vis-à-vis each other. Allowances would not have much impact on these conditions. In short, it is difficult to conceive how a family allowance program reaching all children might, in modern American circumstances, reduce wages. It is even more difficult to imagine how preschool allowances might reduce wages. During two thirds of a child's life, the wage earner would be supporting him without any allowance.*

A few words should be said about the administration of the program. The conditions of eligibility are simple—name, birth date, parent's or guardian's name and address. The program would be essentially a bookkeeping and clerical operation. Provision may need to be made for cases in which there is a question

---

* In proposing a family allowance program for all children, one would consider reducing or at least not further increasing current allowances for dependent children in various social security programs. For example, with a family allowance program, unemployment insurance benefits would not be so inadequate for families with several children as they are now. As the proposal we are considering is limited to young children, however, we cannot consider that it disposes of the need for family benefits in social security.

as to whether funds have been used properly. The question whether funds would actually be used for children arises in relation to family allowances more frequently than with other programs. Perhaps other programs are envisaged as having a supervisory staff and family allowances imagined in the simplest possible terms. At any rate, in the carrying out of none of the programs developed abroad has neglect of children or misuse of funds been found to be a serious problem—not in the family allowance programs of Canada or France,[170] not in the fatherless, child insurance program of New Zealand,[218] and not in the negative income tax program of Denmark. Such problems as arise seem likely to involve a very small percentage of families.

In the United States the protection of children is assumed basically by local and state governments. Whether an agency administering benefits for children should specifically safeguard the payment in relation to the child depends upon the philosophy of the program. The income tax provides a benefit for children, but no one suggests that the Internal Revenue Service investigate whether particular children benefit. The Social Security Act provides for a payment to be made to a relative or other person if it appears that a beneficiary's best interests would be served. A similar provision might be written into a new program, particularly if the sums involved were substantial. The provision could be administered through the agency's own field staff or through an arrangement with local child protective agencies.

One other administrative question arises: Should the father or mother receive the payment? In the case of fatherless child insurance, the payment is received by the parent who has the children—usually the mother. In a program of NEGIT, the person who files for the family would automatically receive the payment. As the choice is left to the family, presumably the payee would usually be the father. As for family allowances, many countries make the payment to the mother; this practice emphasizes the special intent of the family allowance and where necessary safeguards the money for children. It might be argued that payment to the mother interferes with the father's conception of himself as the family head and wage earner.[168] However, the special purpose of the allowance and the special responsibility of mothers for it would probably be widely understood, even by men whose self-regard was vulnerable.

ALTERNATIVE LINE OF PROGRAM DEVELOPMENT

Preschool allowance payments may be in such amounts as to encourage poor families to take off. But this can happen only if two kinds of calculated costs are accepted, both of which arise from wiping out income tax exemptions for all children. In the first place, families with comparatively high incomes would show a net loss compared to their current situation. Although it may be practical to try to favor poor children in distributing the *additional* wealth that the nation accrues from year to year, it may be impractical to try to accomplish this out of what the nation has at any given moment. In other words, it may be impractical to try to give poor children more by giving rich children less. In the second place, even though families with moderate or middle incomes would show a net gain over a period of eighteen years, it might seem unfair to expect them to forego both family allowances and income tax exemptions while they are supporting school-age and still dependent children. The situation is particularly unfair for poor families with school-age children. They will pay little in taxes, but that little will seem much.

Both objections may be met by provision of a family allowance that pays $25 a month for each child up to six years of age and $10 a month for each child between six and eighteen. In effect, families would receive—in exchange for yielding the income tax exemption—at least the equivalent of a $600 exemption

163

at a 20 per cent rate of tax. The net cost of this proposal would be smaller, about $4 billion. Poor children would receive a fairer share of the national income, as they would under a program of preschool allowances.* However, the alternative proposal does not contain the most attractive feature of a preschool allowance program—a payment large enough to assure poor families surplus income at a critical point in the family-income cycle. At $25 a month, only one out of four preschool children would be brought out of poverty. Only a handful of children would be members of families with surplus as large as $650 a year.

One may nevertheless regard the "$25 and $10" family allowance as a conservative start toward a more substantial program.

CONCLUSION

The cost of a universal but modest program of family allowances approximates $14 billion. We judge this to be more expensive than is reasonable in terms of its probable impact on childhood poverty. Therefore we have formulated a more substantial program that would benefit directly only children under six years of age—but all children at those ages would be reached. For a highly significant half dozen years, poverty would be averted for three children out of four. The median child for whom poverty was averted in those early years would live in a family with a surplus

---

* The gross cost of the proposal would be $12.7 billion. Seven billion dollars would be recaptured by wiping out the exemption for children under eighteen and an additional $1.7 billion would be collected from taxing the allowance itself.

Of the gross outlay, poor families would receive $2.8 billion. Assuming that loss of the income tax exemption and the tax collected on the family allowance would together represent $300 million, poor families would be receiving a $2.5 billion net increase in income at a net cost of $4 billion. As poor families have 20 per cent of the children, obviously the proposal favors them.

The way the advantage falls is represented in the second table of Appendix III.

of $50 a month over its barest needs. For the remaining children in those first half dozen years and for many school children later on, poverty would be alleviated but not averted.

The program would provide a powerful push toward the achievement of a decent income and family stability in the first years of marriage. From a variety of points of view—when the mother is encouraged to work, when it provides surplus income, when encouraging intact families—it promotes exactly the patterns that may lead to take-off. The program would not represent as significant a force in the early careers of *middle*-income families but nevertheless would tend to add to the quality of their children's care. When children arrive at school age, the program would end. This is its major drawback. This drawback might be compensated for if preschool allowances are seen in tandem with the development of public services delivered through schools and community centers. Finally, the proposal as formulated would tend to give to children now poor a larger share in the nation's resources.

In comparing the merits of preschool allowances with the first two proposals, it is important to bear in mind that preschool allowances carry the largest cost figure, one almost twice that for a negative income tax. A cost limitation is imposed upon NEGIT by the incentive problem and upon fatherless child insurance by the program's definition. NEGIT has a limitation on benefit levels that cannot be circumvented and FCI a built-in limitation on coverage. According to point of view, one reads these limitations as advantages or disadvantages.

10

Conclusion

✠✠✠✠✠✠✠✠✠✠✠✠✠✠✠✠✠✠✠✠✠

Sixteen million poor children are 16 million too many. Whatever our problems—and we have them to work out—we have the resources to see that no child in the United States is poor. We are rich enough to wipe out poverty of the nineteenth-century variety: rats, rags, and rickets. We can now complete the task. Because our standard of living is rising so rapidly we are in a position—without perceptible cost to any individual—to wipe out poverty of the twentieth-century variety: evidenced when any child has dramatically less of life's goods than the average child has. Whether the antagonist is nineteenth- or twentieth-century poverty, we have the will to act and the resources that are required.

An income maintenance program for children is only one component of national policy, but it is an inescapable component. Money does not in itself teach; neither do schools in themselves feed and shelter. Three out of four children now poor have suffered or will suffer in terms of *income* from membership in a broken family or a large family. It is impractical to conceive of reaching them adequately through the normal route of earnings or programs intended to correct for interrupted earnings.

We have outlined a method for evaluating an income maintenance program. The method begins with understanding the way poor people live. We have reviewed a theory, or at any rate a hypothesis, that the family and income cycle is not two events but one. Money can be fitted into the family-income career so that it merely sustains; less we may not do. With enough money and thoughtfulness, money can be fitted in so that it provides the opportunity for take-off.

Put most simply, poor people need from money for self-improvement what all people need: to be able to count on the income that seems to be theirs and to find in or around it some room for maneuver. They need income that is dependable and provides or permits "social capital." Such income might be particularly useful at two identifiable periods in the family-income cycle. The two periods are the half dozen years around the time a family starts out and the later time when it contains teenage youngsters. Phrased differently, one may expect to help preschool children by focusing on the resources of their parents. With teenagers one looks forward to influencing their own family-income cycle by focusing on their own resources.

167

A parallel thread is implicit in all our discussion. Because economics and finance are older disciplines and because they have come to seem the most exact of the social sciences, their techniques have dominated choices in national policy. Perhaps, also, the daily need for subsistence is basically economic; if we carry primordial memories at all, the primacy of food must be one of them. Now we are affluent. We can begin to make choices *primarily* on grounds other than what contributes to national growth. This assertion, although it has been made before,* provokes scant response if we cannot visualize techniques for judging the quality of life. We have proposed one technique in this book—to examine the impact of given programs on the way families live and develop. The body we built for this notion may be frail and wan, but in the third decade of American affluence the need to appraise national policy in terms other than production cannot be dodged.

As we approach the development of an income maintenance program, particularly one based on the assumptions that have been stated, we are troubled by a pervasive dilemma. Our basic wish is to direct resources to poor families. Yet when we devise programs for poor families alone, we tend to load them with restrictive conditions and frequently we stigmatize the helpless beneficiaries. A recent national experience of this sort was described as follows by Richard Titmuss:

> This [poor law] system, which legally survived in Britain until 1948, inevitably involved personal discrimination. The stigmata of the poor law test, moral judgments by people about other people and their behavior, were a condition of redistribution. The requirements of poor law and public assistance administration were, we can now see, remarkably attuned to the character-

---

* By John Galbraith, for example. He wrote that "all of the conditions for a shift from the primary preoccupation with unemployment and growth do exist. The primary prescription must henceforth be for what may broadly be called the quality of life. This is now the primary goal." [66]

istics of bureaucracy. . . . It was theoretically a neat and orderly world of eligible and ineligible citizens; of approved and disapproved patterns of dependency; of those who could manage change and those who could not. From its operation for over a century Britain inherited in 1948 a whole set of administrative attitudes, values and rites; essentially middle-class in structure; and moralistic in application. The new social service bottles of 1948 had poured into them much of the old wine of discrimination and prejudice.[191]

The alternative to pouring the old wine of the poor law into new bottles is to proceed with expansion of the universal social insurances. Unfortunately, as we have shown, social insurance may omit large numbers of the poorest people. In the dilemma one may plump for a program for poor people or for a universal program, arguing in either case that this time we shall not repeat the historic injustices. The three proposals that have been presented permit one to opt either way. The negative income tax is a program for poor people; fatherless child insurance and pre-school allowances are in the tradition of universal social insurance. We have not developed a resolution to this dilemma. We have merely tried to formulate NEGIT so that it stands the greatest chance of escaping the history of poor laws. We have tried to formulate the social insurance programs so that they benefit poor people especially.

We have by-passed one conceivable resolution of the problem. A proposal such as that of Lady Rhys-Williams would call for a universal payment to all citizens. We have taken this to be an impractical proposal for this decade or the next, and we have not evaluated it. We have judged the country to be unprepared to guarantee income in ways not somehow related to situation or age or work history. But our wealth grows and our humanity with it. Who knows how long this judgment will hold? In any event, our concern here is for children. We are a child-centered country; yet in income maintenance we have done least of all for

169

our children. It is the modest objective of this book to set out to rectify this deficiency.

We have been obstructed at every turn by a perverse quality that may be identified, if it cannot be avoided. No matter how we conceive a program (with the possible exception of NEGIT), we cannot funnel a precise amount of money precisely to the people who need it. Many problems complicate the simple impulse: Poor children live with parents and other adults. Income is a family affair; we cannot consider the children as rescued if the family is poor. The situation of poor people does not stand still. A program may itself induce a mother to give up employment and thus need more income. We are deliberately trying to keep children from working as early as some now do. Thus the initiation of a program may produce conditions that will increase its cost. We wish to avoid a means test; but in moving to any form of averaging need, we inevitably increase the cost. And so on. Current income maintenance programs represent "40 per cent of the income of the poor population, yet most of such income goes to the nonpoor. . . ." [104] Programs of social security were devised to do more than prevent poverty. Here we observe that even when we deliberately frame programs to deal only with poverty, they all cost more than a simple static weighing of need might suggest. As we have learned in many other ways, resources are one problem and a satisfactory system of distributing them is a separate, stubborn problem.

Still, the additional money that is spent is not lost. If we make our choices consciously and thoughtfully, we achieve objectives such as the gaining of self-respect and dignity that do not inevitably accompany the provision of money. Moreover, the effects of the program spread far beyond children. If we eliminated poverty for families with children in 1964, fewer than a third of those counted poor would remain poor. (Almost 10 million adults are members of families with poor children.) We should then be concerned with a remainder of about 10 million adults, some in families and some living alone. More than half of the 10 million are aged; others are disabled, unemployed, and so forth.[138] It becomes evident that most of those who would remain poor could be reached through improvement of existing social security mechanisms. (We do not overlook here the significance of preparing for and providing employment. Unemployment, partial employment, and low wages obviously place a heavy load on any system of income maintenance.)

The costs of the proposals, as they work out, are generally below 1 per cent of current annual national income. Where the option to consider a much higher cost presented itself—in the discussion of family allowances—we took the conservative course. Therefore none of the proposals succeeds in wiping out need among all children. Neither does any of the proposals, unaided, answer the challenge of the third chapter—regularly to provide enough and more than enough income for all or almost all children during both periods that determine their futures.

Because these proposals are not sufficiently powerful, taken alone, any one of them must count on tying in with other efforts, public and personal. We have noted what might be done through school and community services. We have rejected the temptation to assume that AFDC would diminish because of one of these new programs. On the contrary, some lines along which AFDC might be improved have at least been touched on. Finally, we have assumed that families would continue to make their own efforts to produce income. In particular, the incentive for men to work should not be undermined and mothers, once their children are in school, may plan to earn their own income.

When we compare the specific programs for children that have been considered, it must be evident that no single program proves pre-eminently suitable. The negative income tax achieves coverage of all poor children, but not well; it mitigates, it does not correct. Fatherless child insurance does comparatively well for those it reaches; it leaves too many untouched. A preschool

171

allowance reaches more poor children than fatherless child insurance but not so many as NEGIT. With the children it succeeds in reaching, a preschool allowance is more effective than the negative income tax but less effective than fatherless child insurance. We have reviewed other effects of these programs—on the incentive to work, on the distribution of income in the country, on family patterns. A checklist (Appendix V) would find no single program meeting all specifications.

The solution need not lie exclusively in one program or another. A moment's reflection will make it clear that the degree of social security we have so far achieved rests on the relationship of scores of disparate national programs. The most compelling question may be whether a particular income maintenance program best fills the most urgent need. Then, does it fit in with our conception of existing services, of public services, and of income from earnings to achieve the objective we seek?

If this observation is taken as releasing anyone from the need to choose among the programs that have been presented, it is not sufficiently understood. Three programs have been defined that would, more or less effectively, do away with need among children. No one may call himself guiltless who turns away from all these programs unless he knows how we shall achieve the objective. The objective, it should be remembered, is to assure to all children a sense of adequacy and to prepare them to have power freely to govern their adult lives. In our book, these derive from being assured a fair share in the fruits of an ever more prosperous nation.

APPENDIXES

✠✠✠✠✠✠✠✠✠✠✠✠✠✠✠✠✠✠✠

APPENDIX I *Gross Reproduction Rate,*[a] *United States and Canada, 1926–62*

YEAR	U.S.	CANADA	YEAR	U.S.	CANADA
			1945	1212.	1462.
1926	1370.	1628.	46	1430.	1640.
27	1365.	1609.	47	1593.	1753.
28	1305.	1604.	48	1514.	1676.
29	1245.	1565.	49	1515.	1678.
1930	1245.	1599.	1950	1505.	1678.
31	1181.	1555.	51	1593.	1701.
32	1140.	1499.	52	1637.	1763.
33	1074.	1394.	53	1668.	1812.
34	1108.	1368.	54	1727.	1861.
1935	1091.	1346.	1955	1745.	1863.
36	1071.	1310.	56	1798.	1874.
37	1085.	1286.	57	1837.	1907.
38	1113.	1314.	58	1807.	1886.
39	1088.	1294.	59	1812.	1915.
1940	1121.	1348.	1960	1803.	1893.
41	1168.	1377.	61	1790.	1868.
42	1277.	1434.	62	1714.	1836.
43	1323.	1478.			
44	1249.	1457.			

Source: U.S. National Center for Health Statistics.

[a] The gross reproduction rate is the average number of daughters a hypothetical cohort of women starting life together would bear if they all survived from birth to the end of the child-bearing period and if they experienced a given set of age-specific fertility rates. Usually this measure is computed from fertility rates in a single calendar year. It is often interpreted as showing the extent to which the generation of daughters would replace the generation of mothers if fertility remained constant at a given level and if there were no deaths.

175

APPENDIX II *Number of Poor Families That Would Receive Negative Income Tax Payments under Proposal, by Number of Payments per Family, 1963*

	HUSBAND-WIFE FAMILIES WITH					
NUMBER OF PAYMENTS	ONE CHILD	TWO CHILDREN	THREE CHILDREN	FOUR CHILDREN	FIVE CHILDREN	SIX OR MORE CHILDREN
1	583,000	210,000	217,000	76,000	14,000	—
2		357,000	135,000	136,000	76,000	15,000
3			273,000	88,000	67,000	72,000
4				155,000	75,000	74,000
5					154,000	86,000
6 or more						202,000

	FEMALE-HEADED FAMILIES WITH					
NUMBER OF PAYMENTS	ONE CHILD	TWO CHILDREN	THREE CHILDREN	FOUR CHILDREN	FIVE CHILDREN	SIX OR MORE CHILDREN
1	317,000	92,000	40,000	17,000	4,000	—
2		248,000	64,000	35,000	14,000	12,000
3			227,000	40,000	5,000	10,000
4				101,000	15,000	19,000
5					90,000	25,000
6 or more						86,000

Source: Calculations are based on Table 4 in Mollie Orshansky, "Who's Who among the Poor: A Demographic View of Poverty," *Social Security Bulletin*, Vol. 28, No. 7 (July 1965).[139]

APPENDIX III *Number of Poor Families That Would Receive Family Allowance Payments, by Number of Children, if $50 a Month Were Paid for Every Child under the Age of Eighteen*[a]

FAMILIES WITH CHILDREN	TOTAL	STILL POOR	NO LONGER POOR
All families	4,748	1,906	2,842
With 1 child	1,045	695	350
With 2 children	978	474	504
With 3 children	962	413	549
With 4 children	648	178	470
With 5 children	514	146	368
With 6 or more children	601	—	601
TOTAL NUMBER OF CHILDREN	15,256	4,324	10,932
PER CENT	100	28.3	71.7

Amount Family Income Exceeds Poverty Level for Families No Longer Poor[a]

FAMILIES WITH CHILDREN	$0–499	$500–999	$1,000–1,499	$1,500–1,999	$2,000 and Over
All families	1,009	706	494	297	335
With 1 child	340	10	—	—	—
With 2 children	224	265	15	—	—
With 3 children	147	171	213	18	—
With 4 children	89	104	136	127	14
With 5 children	83	70	67	62	86
With 6 or more children	126	87	63	90	235

Source: Calculations are based on Table 4 in Mollie Orshansky, "Who's Who among the Poor: A Demographic View of Poverty," *Social Security Bulletin*, Vol. 28, No. 7 (July 1965).[139]
[a] Proportions arrived at from a hypothetical program applying to all children

Illustrative Effects on Income of a Family Allowance Paying $300/Yr to Children 0–5 and $120/Yr to Children 6–18

FAMILY OF TWO PARENTS AND	ANNUAL BENEFIT	NET CHANGE ANNUALLY FROM CURRENT SITUATION		
		AT MARGIN OF POVERTY	AT $2,000	AT $8,000
1 Child under 6	$300	+$194	+$216	+$129
3 Children under 6	900	+ 500	+ 760	+ 360
1 Child under 6 and 3 Children 6–18	660	+ 257	+ 568	+ 48
4 Children 6–18	480	+ 92	+ 413	– 96

are used in the text to estimate the coverage and impact of a program applying only to children under six. The proportions are used without alteration for the first years of marriage, when it may be assumed that children under six are in fact all children. As applied to all families, comparison with another set of calculations cited in the text suggests that proportions based on an allowance to all children represent a 50 per cent overstatement. The calculation of the amount by which family income exceeds the poverty level is, therefore, also taken to be a 50 per cent overstatement and adjusted downward in applying it to the effects of the preschool allowance.

APPENDIX IV *System of Basic Income Allowances*

An excerpt from an article by James Tobin, "On Improving the Economic Status of the Negro," in *Daedalus*, Vol. 94, No. 4 (Fall 1965).[193]

The defects of present categorical assistance programs could be, in my opinion, greatly reduced by adopting a system of basic income allowances, integrated with and administered in conjunction with the federal income tax. In a sense the proposal is to make the income tax symmetrical. At present the federal government takes a share of family income in excess of a certain amount (for example, a married couple with three children pays no tax unless their income exceeds $3,700). The proposal is that the Treasury pay any family who falls below a certain income a fraction of the shortfall. The idea has sometimes been called a negative income tax.

The payment would be a matter of right, like an income tax refund. Individuals expecting to be entitled to payments from the government during the year could receive them in periodic installments by making a declaration of expected income and expected tax withholdings. But there would be a final settlement between the individual and the government based on a "tax" return after the year was over, just as there is now for taxpayers on April 15.

A family with no other income at all would receive a basic allowance scaled to the number of persons in the family. For a concrete example, take the basic allowance to be $400 per year per person. It might be desirable and equitable, however, to reduce the additional basic allowance for children after, say, the fourth. Once sufficient effort is being made to disseminate birth control knowledge and technique, the scale of allowances by family size certainly should provide some disincentive to the creation of large families.

A family's allowance would be reduced by a certain fraction of every dollar of other income it received. For a concrete example, take this fraction to be one third. This means that the family has considerable incentive to earn income, because its total income including allowances will be increased by two thirds of whatever it earns. In contrast, the means test connected with present public

179

Appendixes

assistance is a 100 per cent "tax" on earnings. With a one-third "tax" a family will be on the receiving end of the allowance and income tax system until its regular income equals three times its basic allowance.

Families above this "break-even" point would be taxpayers. But the less well-off among them would pay less taxes than they do now. The first dollars of income in excess of this break-even point would be taxed at the same rate as below, one third in the example. At some income level, the tax liability so computed would be the same as the tax under the present income tax law. From that point up, the present law would take over; taxpayers with incomes above this point would not be affected by the plan.

The best way to summarize the proposal is to give a concrete graphical illustration. On the horizontal axis of Figure 1 is measured family income from wages and salaries, interest, dividends, rents, and so forth—"adjusted gross income" for the Internal Revenue Service. On the vertical axis is measured the corresponding "disposable income," that is, income after federal taxes and allowances. If the family neither paid taxes nor received allowance, disposable income would be equal to family income; in the diagram this equality would be shown by the 45° line from the origin. Disposable income above this 45° line means the family receives allowances; disposable income below this line means the family pays taxes. The broken line OAB describes the present income tax law for a married couple with three children, allowing the standard deductions. The line CD is the revision which the proposed allowance system would make for incomes below $7,963. For incomes above $7,963, the old tax schedule applies.

Beneficiaries under Federal Old Age Survivors and Disability Insurance would not be eligible for the new allowances. Congress should make sure that minimum benefits under OASDI are at least as high as the allowances. Some government payments, especially those for categorical public assistance, would eventually be replaced by basic allowances. Others, like unemployment insurance and veterans' pensions, are intended to be rights earned by past services regardless of current need. It would therefore be wrong to withhold

180

allowances from the beneficiaries of these payments, but it would be reasonable to count them as income in determining the size of allowances, even though they are not subject to tax.

Although the numbers used above are illustrative, they are indicative of what is needed for an effective program. It would be expensive for the federal budget, involving an expenditure of perhaps fifteen billion dollars a year. Partially offsetting this budgetary cost are the savings in public assistance, on which governments now spend five and six-tenths billion dollars a year, of which three and two-tenths billion are federal funds. Also, savings are possible in a host of other income maintenance programs, notably in agriculture.

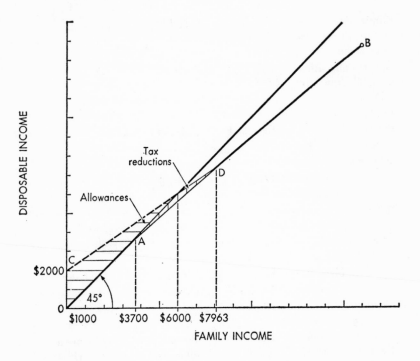

FIGURE 1. Illustration of proposed income allowance plan (married couple with three children)

181

APPENDIX V

A checklist comparing the three programs on various qualities oversimplifies them and is more susceptible to bias than carefully qualified statements. With these cautions in mind, the checklist is offered as a mnemonic device.

EFFECTIVENESS IN	NEGATIVE INCOME TAX	FATHERLESS CHILD INSURANCE	PRESCHOOL ALLOWANCE
Coverage	Excellent	Fair	Excellent, for preschool children only; absent for other children
Eliminating poverty and providing surplus income	Very poor	Good	Very good
Efficient allocation of public funds to poor people	Excellent	Fair	Good
Fairer shares for poor children	Excellent	Fair	Good
Effect on men's incentive to work	Little, if any	None	None
Effective on women's incentive to work	Little, if any	Neutral	Neutral when there are preschool children. Encourages work later
Effect on family stability	Marginal to good	Excellent	Excellent
Effect on birth rate	Little, if any	Little, if any	Little, if any
Encouragement to postpone beginning families	Marginal effect	Good	No effect
Long-range reactions toward receiving benefits	Debatable	Benefits are an earned right	Benefits are a citizen's right
COST	$3.5 billion	$4 billion	$5.9 billion

References

1. Abbott, Edith. Acceptance Speech at Presentation of Survey Award. *The Social Welfare Forum, 1951.* New York: Columbia University Press, 1951.

2. ————. "Public Assistance—Whither Bound?" *Proceedings of the National Conference of Social Work.* Indianapolis, 1937, p. 7.

3. Advisory Council on Public Assistance. *Public Assistance.* Washington, D.C., Government Printing Office, January 1960, pp. 30–32.

4. AFL-CIO Executive Council. Miami, February 1956.

5. Ainsworth, Mary D., *et al. Deprivation of Maternal Care: A Reassessment of Its Effect.* World Health Organization. Public Health Papers, No. 14, 1962.

6. Aller, Curtis C. "Towards the Prevention of Dependency: A Report on AFDCU Recipients." Preliminary report. Dittoed, 1965, pp. 16, 18.

7. Becker, Joseph M. (ed.). *In Aid of the Unemployed.* "The Adequacy of Benefits in Unemployment Insurance." Baltimore: Johns Hopkins Press, 1965.

8. Beresford, John, and Alice Rivlin. "Characteristics of 'Other' Families." Paper read at the Population Association of America, Philadelphia. Dittoed, April 19, 1963.

9. Bernard, Jessie. *Remarriage: A Study of Marriage.* New York: Dryden Press, 1956.

10. Bernard, Sydney E. *The Economic and Social Adjustment of Low-Income Female-Headed Families.* Waltham, Mass.: Brandeis University. Mimeographed, May 1964.

11. Beveridge, Sir William. *Social Insurance and Allied Services.* New York: Macmillan Co., 1942, p. 134.

12. Blau, Peter M. *The Dynamics of Bureaucracy.* Chicago: University of Chicago Press, 1955.

References

13. Blood, Robert O., Jr. "The Husband-Wife Relationship." In F. Ivan Nye, *The Employed Mother in America.*

14. Bowen, W. G., and T. A. Finegan. "Labor Force Participation and Unemployment." Princeton Industrial Relations Section. Mimeographed, undated.

15. Bowerman, Charles E., Donald P. Irish, and Hallowell Pope. *Unwed Motherhood: Personal and Social Consequences.* Chapel Hill, N.C.: University of North Carolina. Unpublished, 1965.

16. Bowlby, John. *Maternal Care and Mental Health.* World Health Organization. Monograph Series, No. 2, 1952.

17. Boyden, William C. "The Property Aspects of Divorce." *Conference on Divorce.* Law School of the University of Chicago, February 29, 1952.

18. Brady, Dorothy S. *Age and the Income Distribution.* Social Security Administration. Research Report No. 8, Washington, D.C.: Government Printing Office, 1965.

19. Burchinal, Lee G. "Research on Young Marriage: Implications for Family Life Education." In Marvin B. Sussman, *Sourcebook in Marriage and the Family.* Boston: Houghton Mifflin, 1963, p. 519.

20. Burgess, M. Elaine, and Daniel O. Price. *An American Dependency Challenge.* Chicago: American Public Welfare Association, 1963.

21. Burns, Eveline M. *Social Security and Public Policy.* New York: McGraw-Hill, 1956.

22. ———. "Social Security in Evolution: Towards What?" Address to the American Economic Association. Chicago, December 1964, p. 5. Also in *The Social Service Review*, June 1965.

23. ———. "Welfare Programs in Evolution." *Monthly Labor Review.* Vol. 88, No. 3 (March 1965).

24. Butler, Senator Hugh. "Program for a True Pay-as-You-Go Full-coverage Social Security System." *Congressional Record.* June 16, 1950, October 20, 1950, January 17, 1951.

25. State of California. Department of Social Welfare. *First Annual Report.* January 1965, Table 20.

26. Callaghan, Hubert Curtis. *The Family Allowance Procedure.* A Ph.D. dissertation submitted to the School of Social Science

of the Catholic University of America. Catholic University of America Press, 1947.

27. Campbell, Arthur A. "Recent Fertility Trends in the United States and Canada." Paper presented to the United Nations World Population Conference. Belgrade, Yugoslavia, August 30 to September 10, 1965.

28. Carter, Hugh, and Alexander Plateris. "Trends in Divorce and Family Disruption." *Health, Education, and Welfare Indicators.* Department of Health, Education, and Welfare, September 1963.

29. Christensen, Harold T. "Studies in Child-Spacing: I. Premarital Pregnancy as Measured by the Spacing of the First Birth from Marriage." *American Sociological Review,* February 1953.

30. ———, and Hanna H. Meissner. "Premarital Pregnancy as a Factor in Divorce." In Robert F. Winch, Robert McGinnis, and Herbert R. Barringer. *Selected Studies in Marriage and the Family.* New York: Holt, Rinehart, and Winston, 1963.

31. *Cleveland Press,* December 2, 1964.

32. Cohen, Wilbur J., William Haber, and Eva Mueller. *The Impact of Unemployment in the 1958 Recession.* U.S. Senate. Special Committee on Unemployment Problems. Washington, D.C.: Government Printing Office, June 1960.

33. Colm, Gerhard. "The Economic Base and Limits of Social Welfare." *Monthly Labor Review.* Vol. 6, No. 6 (June 1963).

34. Committee on Economic Security. *Report to the President of the Committee on Economic Security.* Washington, D.C.: Government Printing Office, 1935, pp. 3, 5.

35. Conference on Economic Progress. *Poverty and Deprivation in the United States.* Washington, D.C. 1962.

36. Coombs, Lolagene C. "Child Spacing and Family Economic Position." Unpublished memorandum dated May 31, 1965, for a study conducted by Ronald Freedman and Lolagene C. Coombs. "Economic Status, Employment, and Family Growth." Ann Arbor: University of Michigan.

37. Corkey, Elizabeth C. "A Family Planning Program for the Low Income Family." *Journal of Marriage and the Family.* Vol. 26, No. 4 (November 1964), p. 480.

38. Corley, Francis J. *Family Allowances.* St. Louis: Institute of Social Order, 1947.

185

39. Cutright, Phillips. "A Pilot Study of Factors in Economic Success or Failure." Social Security Administration. Processed, 1964.

40. Davidson, George F. "Canada's Family Allowances in Retrospect." *Children*. Vol. 4, No. 3 (May–June 1957).

41. Davidson, P. E., and H. D. Anderson. *Occupational Mobility in an American Community*. Stanford, Calif.: Stanford University Press, 1937.

42. Davis, Joseph S. "Implications of Prospective United States Population Growth in the 1960's." *The Milbank Memorial Fund Quarterly*. Vol. 39, No. 2 (April 1961).

43. Douglas, Paul H. *Wages and the Family*. Chicago: University of Chicago Press, 1927, pp. 253 and ix.

44. Dumpson, James R. "The Economy of Adequate Service." *Child Welfare*. Vol. XXXIX, No. 10 (December 1960).

45. Duncan, Otis Dudley. "Farm Background and Differential Fertility." *Demography*. Vol. 2 (1965).

46. Easterlin, Richard A. "The Baby Boom in Perspective." *American Economic Review* (December 1961).

47. ———. "On the Relation of Economic Factors to the Recent Fertility Decline." Meeting of the Population Association of America. Chicago, April 23, 1965.

48. *Economic Report of the President, Together with the Annual Report of the Council of Economic Advisers*. Washington, D.C.; Government Printing Office, January 1964, pp. 77–78.

49. Edstrom, Eve. "They're All Scufflin'—Like Me." *Washington Post*. January 12, 1964.

50. Eldridge, Hope T. *Population Policies: A Survey of Recent Developments*. Washington, D.C.: International Union for the Scientific Study of Population, 1954, pp. 121 and 47.

51. Epstein, Abraham. *Insecurity—A Challenge to America*. New York: Random House, 1938.

52. Epstein, Lenore A. "Some Effects of Low Income on Children and Their Families." *Social Security Bulletin*. Vol. 24, No. 2 (February 1961).

53. Erikson, Erik H. *Childhood and Society*. New York: W. W. Norton, 1950.

54. ———. *Young Man Luther.* New York: W. W. Norton, 1958.

55. ———. "Youth and the Life Cycle." *Children.* Vol. 7, No. 2 (March–April 1960), p. 48.

56. "Evicted Children." *Washington Post.* April 9, 1965. Editorial page.

57. Febvay, M. "Niveau et évolution de la fécondité par catégorie socio-professionelle en France." *Population.* Vol. 14, No. 4 (October–December 1959).

58. Fields, Theron J. "Company-Initiated Early Retirement as a Means of Work-Force Control." Mimeographed, Cornell University, December 1963.

59. Fine, S. A. *The Nature of Automated Jobs and Their Educational and Training Requirements.* A Report for the Office of Manpower, Automation, and Training. U.S. Department of Labor. Processed June 1964.

60. Folger, John K. and Charles B. Nam. "Trends in Education in Relation to the Occupational Structure." *Sociology of Education.* Vol. 38, No. 1 (Fall 1964).

61. Freedman, Deborah. "The Relation of Economic Status to Fertility." *American Economic Review.* Vol. LIII, No. 3 (June 1963).

62. Freedman, Ronald. "The Sociology of Human Fertility: A Trend Report and Bibliography." *Current Sociology.* Vol. X–XI, No. 2 (1961–62), pp. 53, 59.

63. ———, and Lolagene Coombs. "Working Paper on Family Income and Family Growth." June 1963. Appendix B and Appendix C, "Working Paper on Changes in the Family Situation."

64. ———, Pascal K. Whelpton and Arthur A. Campbell. *Family Planning, Sterility and Population Growth.* New York: McGraw-Hill, 1959.

65. Friedman, Milton. *Capitalism and Freedom.* Chicago: University of Chicago Press, 1962.

66. Galbraith, John Kenneth. "On the Quality of Life." *Encounter.* Vol. XXIV, No. 1 (January 1965).

67. Galloway, Lowell E. "The Retirement Decision: An Exploratory Essay." Social Security Administration. Research Report No. 9, 1965.

References

68. Geismar, Ludwig L. and Michael A. La Sorte. *Understanding the Multi-Problem Family*. New York: Association Press, 1964.

69. Gendell, Murray. *Swedish Working Wives. A Study of Determinants and Consequences*. A Ph.D. thesis. Totowa, N.J.: Bedminster Press, 1963.

70. Glick, Paul C. *American Families*. New York: John Wiley and Sons, 1957.

71. ———. "Marriage Instability: Variations by Size of Place and Region." *The Milbank Memorial Fund Quarterly*. January 1963.

72. ———. "Stability of Marriage in Relation to Age at Marriage." In Robert F. Winch, Robert McGinnis, and Herbert R. Barringer. *Selected Studies in Marriage and the Family*. New York: Holt, Rinehart, and Winston, 1963.

73. ———, David M. Heer and John Beresford. "Family Formation and Family Composition: Trends and Prospects." In Marvin B. Sussman (ed.), *Sourcebook in Marriage and the Family*. Boston: Houghton Mifflin, 1963.

74. Gordon, Margaret S. *The Economics of Welfare Policies*. New York: Columbia University Press, 1963.

75. Grant, Margaret. *Old-Age Security, Social and Financial Trends*. A Report prepared for the Committee on Social Security. Social Science Research Council. Washington, D.C., 1939, pp. 3–4.

76. Greenleigh Associates. *Facts, Fallacies, and Future*. New York, 1960, p. 98.

77. Groves, Harold M. *Federal Tax Treatment and the Family*. Washington, D.C.: Brookings Institution, 1963.

78. Heberle, R. "Social Factors in Birth Control." *American Sociological Review*. Vol. 6, No. 6 (December 1941).

79. Hildebrand, George H. "The Negative Income Tax and the Problem of Poverty." Cornell University. Mimeographed, undated.

80. Hillman, Karen G. "Mental Instability and Its Relation to Education, Income, and Occupation: An Analysis Based on Census Data." In Robert F. Winch, Robert McGinnis, and Herbert R. Barringer, *Selected Studies in Marriage and the Family*. New York: Holt, Rinehart, and Winston, 1963.

81. Hoffman, Lois Wladis. "Effects on Children . . ." In F. Ivan Nye. *The Employed Mother in America*.

82. Hollingshead, August B. "Trends in Social Stratification: A Case Study." *American Sociological Review.* Vol. 17, No. 6 (December 1952), p. 686.

83. ———, and Frederick C. Redlich. *Social Class and Mental Illness.* New York: John Wiley and Sons, 1958.

84. Hunter, Robert. *Poverty.* New York, 1904.

85. *Les Institutions sociales de la France.* Paris: Documentation Française, 1963, p. 31.

86. Jacobson, Paul H. *American Marriage and Divorce.* New York: Rinehart and Co., 1959.

87. Jaffe, Frederick S. "Family Planning and Poverty." *Journal of Marriage and the Family.* Vol. 26, No. 4 (November 1964).

88. Johnson, Harry G. "The Economics of Poverty: Discussion." Comment on Robert J. Lampman, "Approaches to the Reduction of Poverty." Annual Meeting of the American Economic Association. Chicago, December 30, 1964.

89. Johnston, Denis F. "Educational Attainment of Workers, March 1962." *Monthly Labor Review.* May 1963.

90. Jones, John P. *Remarriage Tables Based on Experience under OASDI and U.S. Employees Compensation Systems.* Social Security Administration. Division of the Actuary. Actuarial Study No. 55, December 1962.

91. Justis, Guy R. Comments on a paper by George Hoshino, "The Means Test Can Be Simplified." National Conference on Social Welfare. Los Angeles, California, May 27, 1964. For small, impressionistic studies of the same issue, see also student research projects by Carl Schier, Irene Schmoke, Janet Spiers, and Ward Zobel, conducted for George Hoshino, University of Pennsylvania School of Social Work, 1965.

92. Kahn, Alfred J. "New Policies and Service Models: The Next Phase." Paper presented at the Annual Meeting, American Orthopsychiatric Association, March 18, 1965.

93. Kantner, John F., and Clyde V. Kiser. "Social and Psychological Factors Affecting Fertility . . ." *The Milbank Memorial Fund Quarterly.* Vol. 32, No. 1 (January 1954).

94. Kaplan, Saul. "Support from Fathers in Aid to Dependent Children." *Social Security Bulletin.* Vol. 21, No. 2 (February 1958).

189

References

95. Keith-Lucas, Alan. *Decisions About People in Need*. Chapel Hill, N.C.: University of North Carolina Press, 1957.

96. Kimmel, Paul R. "A Comparative Study of the Dating and Court-ship Patterns of High School Youth from Low Income Families." Mimeographed, Iowa State University, 1965.

97. Kirk, Dudley. *Europe's Population in the Inter-war Years*. League of Nations, 1946.

98. Klebaner, Benjamin J. "Poverty and Its Relief in American Thought, 1815–61." *Social Service Review*. Vol. 38, No. 4 (December 1964).

99. Komarovsky, Mirra, with the collaboration of Jane H. Philips. *Blue-Collar Marriage*. New York: Random House, 1964, pp. 290, 281.

100. Kronick, Jane C. "Attitudes toward Dependency: A Study of 119 ADC Mothers." Bryn Mawr College, unpublished, May 15, 1963, p. 86.

101. Kubie, Lawrence S. "Provisions for the Care of Children of Divorced Parents: A New Legal Instrument." *Yale Law Journal*. Vol. 73, No. 7 (June 1964).

102. Lampman, Robert J. "Approaches to the Reduction of Poverty." Annual Meeting of the American Economic Association. Chicago, December 30, 1964, p. 8 (Chapter II); p. 5 (Chapter IV).

103. ———. "The Anti-Poverty Program in Historical Perspective." A paper presented to the University of California at Los Angeles faculty "Seminar on Poverty," February 25, 1965, p. 12.

104. ———. "Ends and Means in the War on Poverty." Paper presented at the West Virginia University Conference on "Poverty Amidst Affluence," May 3–7, 1965, p. 12.

105. ———. "Population Change and Poverty-Reduction." Paper presented at the West Virginia University Conference on "Poverty Amidst Affluence," May 3–7, 1965.

106. Lansing, John B., Eva Mueller, William Ladd, and Nancy Barth. *The Geographic Mobility of Labor: A First Report*. Ann Arbor, Mich.: Survey Research Center, April 1963.

107. Lenski, Gerhard. *The Religious Factor*. Garden City, N.Y.: Anchor Books, 1963.

108. Lewis, Hylan, and Camille Jeffers. "Poverty and the Behavior of Low Income Families." Paper presented to the American Orthopsychiatric Association, Chicago, March 19, 1964, p. 11.

109. Lewis, Oscar. *The Children of Sanchez*. New York: Random House, 1961.

110. Lewis, Roscoe. Unpublished report prepared for the Child Rearing Study, Health and Welfare Council of the National Capitol Area. Quoted in the *Washington Post*, January 12, 1964.

111. Lipset, Seymour Martin, and Reinhard Bendix. *Social Mobility in Industrial Society*. Berkeley, Calif.: University of California Press, 1959.

112. Lynes, Tony. "Fiscal Policy and Tax Allowances in Old Age." International Gerontological Seminar. Markaryd, Sweden. Mimeographed, August 6–9, 1963.

113. ———. "A Policy for Family Incomes." *The Listener*. Vol. LXXIII, No. 1878, March 25, 1965, pp. 436–37. Citations offered in evidence on this point are: Neville R. Butler and Dennis G. Bonham, *Perinatal Mortality*, 1963; Royston Lambert, *Nutrition in Britain, 1950–1960*, 1964; London County Council, *Report on the Heights and Weights (and Other Measurements) of School Pupils in the County of London in 1959*, 1961; J. W. B. Douglas, *The Home and School*, 1964.

114. Maas, Henry S., and Richard E. Engler, Jr. *Children in Need of Parents*. New York: Columbia University Press, 1959.

115. Madison, Bernice. "Canadian Family Allowances and their Major Social Implications." *Journal of Marriage and the Family*. Vol. 26, No. 2 (May 1964).

116. Mayer, Anna B. in collaboration with Alfred J. Kahn. *Day Care as a Social Instrument: A Policy Paper*. Columbia University School of Social Work. Mimeographed, January 1965.

117. McClelland, David C. *The Achieving Society*. New York: D. Van Nostrand, 1961.

118. McKeany, Maurine. *The Absent Father and Public Policy in the Program of Aid to Dependent Children*. Berkeley, Calif.: University of California Press, 1960.

119. Meriam, Lewis. *Relief and Social Security*. Washington, D.C.: Brookings Institution, 1946, pp. 840–44.

191

References

120. Miller, Herman P. "Poverty and the Negro." Paper presented at the West Virginia University Conference on "Poverty Amidst Affluence," May 3–7, 1965.

121. ———. *Rich Man, Poor Man*. New York: Thomas Y. Crowell, 1964.

122. ———. *Trends in the Income of Families and Persons in the United States: 1947 to 1960*. U.S. Department of Commerce. Bureau of the Census, 1963.

123. Miller, S. M. "The Outlook of Working-Class Youth." In Arthur B. Shostak and William Gomberg, *Blue Collar World*. Englewood Cliffs, N.J.: Prentice-Hall, 1964.

124. Miller, Walter B. "Implications of Urban Lower-Class Culture for Social Work." *Social Service Review*. September 1959.

125. Mincer, Jacob. "On-the-Job Training: Costs, Returns, and Some Implications." *Journal of Political Economy*. Supplement. Vol. LXX, No. 5, Pt. 2 (October 1962).

126. Monahan, Thomas P. "The Changing Nature and Instability of Remarriages," in Robert F. Winch, Robert McGinnis, and Herbert R. Barringer, *Selected Studies in Marriage and the Family*. New York: Holt, Rinehart, and Winston, 1963.

127. Morgan, Agnes Fay (ed.). *Nutritional Status, U.S.A.* University of California. California Agricultural Experiment Station. Bulletin 769, October 1959.

128. Morgan, James N., Martin H. David, Wilbur J. Cohen, and Harvey E. Brazer. *Income and Welfare in the United States*. New York: McGraw-Hill, 1962, p. 91.

129. Mugge, Robert H. "Aid to Families with Dependent Children: Initial Findings of the 1961 Report on the Characteristics of Recipients." *Social Security Bulletin*. Vol. 26, No. 3 (March 1963).

130. ———. "Children Receiving AFDC." *Welfare in Review*. Vol. 2, No. 3 (March 1964).

131. Myrdal, Alva. *Nation and Family*. New York: Harper and Bros., 1941, pp. 140, 144.

132. "New Patterns in U.S. Fertility." *Population Bulletin*. Vol. XX, No. 5 (September 1964), pp. 114–15.

133. Nye, F. Ivan, and Lois Wladis Hoffman. *The Employed Mother in America*. Chicago: Rand McNally, 1963.

134. Ornati, Oscar. "Poverty in America." Washington, D.C.: National Policy Committee on Pockets of Poverty. Mimeographed, 1964, p. 12.

135. Orshansky, Mollie. "The Aged Negro and His Income." *Social Security Bulletin.* Vol. 27, No. 2 (February 1964).

136. ————. "Children of the Poor." *Social Security Bulletin.* Vol. 26, No. 7 (July 1963).

137. ————. "Children of the Poor: New Dimensions." Paper presented to the National Conference on Social Welfare. Atlantic City, May 24, 1965.

138. ————. "Counting the Poor: Another Look at the Poverty Profile," *Social Security Bulletin.* Vol. 28, No. 1 (January 1965), table 8 and p. 25 (Chapter III) ; table 6 and p. 17 (Chapter X).

139. ————. "Who's Who Among the Poor: A Demographic View of Poverty." *Social Security Bulletin.* Vol. 28, No. 7 (July 1965).

140. Orwell, George. *Down and Out in Paris and London.* London: Victor Gollancz, 1933.

141. Paillat, Paul. "Influence de nombre d'enfants sur le niveau de vie de la famille—évolution de 1950 à 1961." *Population.* No. 3, 1962.

142. Perlman, Helen Harris. "Unmarried Mothers." In Nathan E. Cohen (ed.), *Social Work and Social Problems.* New York: National Association of Social Workers, 1964.

143. Perrella, Vera C., and Forrest A. Bogan. "Out of School Youth, February 1963." *Monthly Labor Review.* Vol. 87, No. 11 (November 1964).

144. "La Population Française, recensement 1962." *Informations Sociales.* Vol. 18, No. 8–9 (August–September 1964).

145. The President's Task Force on Manpower Conservation. *One-Third of a Nation.* January 1, 1964.

146. Pressat, Roland. "La Population Française au recensement de 1962." *Population.* No. 4, 1962, p. 527.

147. Putnam, Israel. *Dimensions of Poverty in 1964.* Office of Economic Opportunity, October 1965, p. 15.

148. Rainwater, Lee. *Family Design.* Chicago: Aldine Publishing Co., 1965, pp. 281–82.

149. ———. "Work and Identity in the Lower Class." Washington University Conference on Planning for the Quality of Urban Life, St. Louis, Mo., November 25, 1964.

150. ———, assisted by Karol Kane Weinstein. *And the Poor Get Children*. Chicago: Quadrangle Books, 1960.

151. Reich, Charles A. "The New Property." *Yale Law Journal*. Vol. 73, No. 5 (April 1964).

152. Reynolds, Lloyd G. *Wages and Labor Mobility in Theory and Practice*. New York: Harper and Bros., 1951, pp. 127–28.

153. Rhys-Williams, Lady Juliet. *Family Allowances and Social Security, Lady Rhys-Williams' Scheme*. London: Liberal Publication Department, 1944.

154. Richmond, Mary E., and Fred S. Hall. *Child Marriages*. New York: Russell Sage Foundation, 1925.

155. Riemer, Ruth, and Clyde V. Kiser. "Social and Psychological Factors Affecting Fertility." *The Milbank Memorial Fund Quarterly*. Vol. 32, No. 2 (April 1954), p. 1050.

156. Riesman, David. "The Search for Challenge." *Kenyon Alumni Bulletin*. January-March 1959.

157. Riessman, Frank. *The Culturally Deprived Child*. New York: Harper and Bros., 1962.

158. Rochefort, Christiane. *Les Petits enfants du siècle*. Paris: Bernard Grasset, 1961.

159. Rohrer, John H., and Munro S. Edmonson, with Harold Lief, Daniel Thompson, and William Thompson. *The Eighth Generation*. New York: Harper and Bros., 1960.

160. Rostow, W. W. *The Stages of Economic Growth*. Cambridge, England: Cambridge University Press, 1960.

161. Roth, Julius A. *Timetables*. Indianapolis: Bobbs-Merrill, 1963.

162. ———, and Robert F. Peck. "Social Class and Social Mobility Factors Related to Marital Adjustment." *American Sociological Review*. Vol. 16, No. 4 (August 1951).

163. Safa, Helen Icken. "The Unwed Mother: A Case Study." Working paper No. 5 in *Fatherless Families: Working Papers*. Youth Development Center, Syracuse University, 1965.

164. Schiffer, Clara G. and Eleanor P. Hunt. *Illness Among Children*.

Welfare Administration. Children's Bureau, Washington, D.C.: Government Printing Office, 1963.

165. Schiffman, Jacob. "Family Characteristics of Workers, 1959." *Monthly Labor Review.* Vol. 84, No. 8 (August 1960).

166. Schorr, Alvin L. *Filial Responsibility in the Modern American Family.* Social Security Administration. Washington, D.C.: Government Printing Office, 1961.

167. ———. "The Non-Culture of Poverty." *American Journal of Orthopsychiatry.* Vol. XXXIV, No. 5 (October 1964).

168. ———. "Problems in the ADC Program." *Social Work.* Vol. 5, No. 2 (April 1960).

169. ———. *Slums and Social Insecurity.* Social Security Administration. Research Report No. 1. Washington, D.C.: Government Printing Office, 1963.

170. ———. *Social Security and Social Services in France.* Social Security Administration. Research Report No. 7, Washington, D.C.: Government Printing Office, 1965.

171. ———, "Towards the Next Step in Social Security: Program for the Social Orphans," *The New York Times Magazine,* March 13, 1966.

172. Schultz, Theodore W. "Investing in Poor People: An Economist's View." *American Economic Review.* Vol. LV, No. 2 (May 1965).

173. Sclanders, Ian. "Bonus for Babies." *The Nation.* February 17, 1964.

174. Sinfield, Adrian. "Unemployed in Tyneside." Mimeographed, Essex, England, May 1964.

175. Smith, Adam. *An Inquiry into the Nature and Causes of the Wealth of Nations.* New York: Modern Library Edition. Random House, 1937, p. 80.

176. Social Scientists' Advisory Meeting, Summary of Deliberations, June 20–21, 1960. Social Security Administration. Mimeographed. Published as "Priorities in Family Life." *Papers in Social Welfare,* No. 3. Waltham, Mass.: Brandeis University.

177. Solow, Robert M. "Technology and Unemployment." *The Public Interest.* Fall 1965, No. 1, p. 23.

178. Somers, Gerald G. "Training the Unemployed." In Joseph M. Becker (ed.), *In Aid of the Unemployed.*

195

References

179. ——— and Ernst W. Stromsdorfer. "A Benefit-Cost Analysis of Manpower Retraining." Chicago: American Economic Association–Industrial Relations Research Association, December 28, 1964.

180. Stein, Robert L. "Work History, Attitudes, and Income of the Unemployed." *Monthly Labor Review.* Vol. 86, No. 12 (December 1963).

181. Stolz, Lois Meek. "Effects of Maternal Employment on Children: Evidence from Research." *Child Development.* Vol. 31 (1960), pp. 749–82.

182. Stone, I. T., D. C. Leighton, and A. H. Leighton. "Poverty and the Individual." Paper presented at the West Virginia University Conference on "Poverty Amidst Affluence," May 3–7, 1965.

183. "Striving for Balance in Community Health and Welfare," New York: State Charities Aid Association, 1963.

184. Surrey, Stanley S. "The Federal Income Tax Base for Individuals." *Columbia Law Review.* Vol. 58, No. 6 (June 1958).

185. ———. "Federal Taxation of the Family—The Revenue Act of 1948." *Harvard Law Review.* Vol. LXI, No. 7 (July 1948), pp. 1097–1164.

186. Swanstrom, Thomas E. "Out-of-School Youth, February 1963, Part II." *Monthly Labor Review.* December 1964.

187. Tawney, R. H. *Equality.* London: George Allen and Unwin, 1952, p. 106.

188. "Taxes on Wages or Employment and Family Allowances in European Countries." *Economic Bulletin for Europe.* Vol. 4, No. 2 (August 1952).

189. tenBroek, Jacobus, and Richard B. Wilson. "Public Assistance and Social Insurance, A Normative Evaluation." *UCLA Law Review.* April 1954.

190. Theobald, Robert. *Free Men and Free Markets.* New York: C. M. Potter, 1963. See also, "The Guaranteed Income: A New Economic and Human Right," Address to the National Conference on Social Welfare," Chicago, May 31, 1966.

191. Titmuss, Richard M. "The Role of Redistribution in Social Policy." *Social Security Bulletin.* Vol. 28, No. 6 (June 1965), pp. 14–20.

192. Titmuss, Richard and Kathleen. *Parents Revolt*. London: Secker and Warburg, 1942, p. 105.

193. Tobin, James, "On Improving the Economic Status of the Negro." *Daedalus*. Vol. 94, No. 4 (Fall 1965).

194. Union Nationale des Caisses d'Allocations Familiales. "Evolution du nombre des familles allocataires, 1948–1963." *Documents*.

195. United Nations. *Demographic Yearbook, 1961*. New York, 1961.

196. U.S. Congress. Joint Committee on the Economic Report. 84th Congress, 1st. Session. *Low Income Families*. Hearings before the Sub-committee on Low Income Families. November 18–23, 1955. Washington, D.C.: Government Printing Office, 1955, p. 144.

197. U.S. Department of Commerce. Bureau of the Census, 1960 census. *Employment Status and Work Experience*. PC(2)–6A, Table 6 (Chapter IV); Table 8 (Chapter IX).

198. ———. ———. *Families*. Final Report, 1960 census PC(2)–4A, Table 35, Table 51 and Table 48.

199. ———. ———. *Historical Statistics of the United States*. Series D26–35. Washington, D.C.: Government Printing Office, 1960.

200. ———. ———. *Occupation by Earnings and Education*, 1960 census, PC(2)–7B, Table 1.

201. ———. ———. *Persons by Family Characteristics*, 1960 census. Final Report. PC(2)–4B, Table 16.

202. ———. ———. *Women by Number of Children Ever Born*. Final Report, 1960 census, PC(2)–3A, Tables 18, 19, 37 and 34 (Chapter III); Tables 37 and 38 (Chapter V).

203. ———. Current Population Reports. *Consumer Income*. Series P–60, No. 43. Washington, D.C.: Government Printing Office, September 29, 1964. Table 22.

204. ———. ———. "Educational Change in a Generation, March 1962." *Population Characteristics*. Series P–20, No. 132. Washington, D.C.: Government Printing Office, September 22, 1964.

205. ———. ———. "Lifetime Occupational Mobility of Adult Males, March 1962." *Technical Studies*. Series P–23, No. 11. Washington, D.C.: Government Printing Office, May 12, 1964.

References

206. U.S. Department of Health, Education, and Welfare. Region II. *Administrative Cost Study, State of New York, Department of Social Welfare, July–October 1959.* New York City. Mimeographed.

207. ———. Public Health Service. National Center for Health Statistics. *Medical Care, Health Status, and Family Income.* Series 10, No. 9. Washington, D.C.: Government Printing Office, May 1964.

208. ———. ———. National Vital Statistics Division. Vital Statistics of the United States 1960. Vol. III, Sections 3, 4, and 7, *Divorces,* Washington, D.C.

209. ———. Social Security Administration. Bureau of Public Assistance. *Illegitimacy and Its Impact on the Aid to Dependent Children Program.* Washington, D.C.: Government Printing Office, April 1960, p. 50.

210. ———. ———. *Widows with Children Under Social Security.* In press.

211. ———. ———. "Population Effects of Income Maintenance." A meeting of demographers at the invitation of the Division of Research and Statistics, April 9, 1965.

212. ———. Welfare Administration. Bureau of Family Services. "Characteristics of Families Receiving Aid to Families with Dependent Children." Mimeographed, April 1963, Table 48.

213. U.S. Department of Labor. U.S. Employment Service. Bureau of Employment Security. "Employment Service Participation in the Labor Market." Washington, D.C.: Government Printing Office, February 1963.

214. ———. *Monthly Labor Review.* Vol. 87, No. 12 (December 1964), Tables A–1 and A–6, Washington, D.C.

215. ———. Women's Bureau. *Negro Women Workers in 1960.* Bulletin 287. Washington, D.C.: Government Printing Office, 1964.

216. Vadakin, James C. *Family Allowances.* Oxford, Ohio: University of Miami Press, 1958, p. 21.

217. Walinsky, Adam. "Keeping the Poor in Their Place." *The New Republic.* July 4, 1964.

218. Watson, W. L. Social Security Commission of New Zealand. Personal communication, August 23, 1961.

219. Westoff, Charles F. "The Changing Focus of Differential Fertility Research: The Social Mobility Hypothesis." *The Milbank Memorial Fund Quarterly*. Vol. 31, No. 1 (January 1953), p. 30.

220. ———. "The Fertility of the American Population." In Ronald Freedman (ed.), *Population: The Vital Revolution*. Chicago: Aldine Publishing Co., 1965.

221. Wickenden, Elizabeth. "Direct Services and Other Benefits in Kind as an Aspect of Income Maintenance Policy." Unpublished paper, August 1, 1964.

222. ———. "The Legal Needs of the Poor, From the Point of View of Public Welfare Policy." Presented at the Conference on "Extension of Legal Services to the Poor," Washington, D.C., November 12, 1964.

223. ———. "Welfare Services." In Joseph M. Becker (ed.), *In Aid of the Unemployed*, p. 263.

224. Wilcock, Richard C. "Who Are the Unemployed" In Joseph M. Becker (ed.), *In Aid of the Unemployed*.

225. Wilensky, Harold L. "The Moonlighter: A Product of Relative Deprivation." *Industrial Relations*. Vol. 3, No. 1 (October 1963), p. 119.

226. ———. "Orderly Careers and Social Participation: The Impact of Work History on Social Integration in the Middle Mass." *American Sociological Review*. Vol. 26, No. 4 (August 1961), p. 522.

227. ———. "Varieties of Work Experience." Berkeley: University of California. Institute of Industrial Relations. Reprint No. 231, 1964.

228. ——— and Hugh Edwards. "The Skidder: Ideological Adjustments of Downward Mobile Workers." *American Sociological Review*. Vol. 24, No. 2 (April 1959).

229. Willard, Joseph W. "Family Allowances in Canada." *International Labor Review*. Vol. LXXV, No. 3 (March 1957), p. 22.

230. ———. "Some Aspects of Family Allowances and Income Redistribution in Canada." *Public Policy*. Vol. V (1954), p. 231.

231. Winston, Ellen. "Educational Approaches to Community Problems." Paper delivered to the Annual Meeting of the Council of National Organizations for Adult Education. Washington, D.C. Mimeographed. December 8, 1964.

References

232. ————. "Implications of the AFDC Eligibility Review." *Welfare in Review*. Vol. 2, No. 7 (July 1964), pp. 5, 7.

233. Wood, Elizabeth. "Knowledge Needed for Adequate Programs of Public and Private Housing." In Donald J. Bogue (ed.), *Needed Urban and Metropolitan Research*. Oxford, Ohio: Miami University Press and Scripps Foundation, 1953, pp. 51–55.

234. Woofter, Thomas J. "Children and Family Income." *Social Security Bulletin*. Vol. 8, No. 1 (January 1945).

235. Wynn, Margaret. *Fatherless Families*. London: Michael Joseph, 1964.

236. Young, Arthur. *Eastern Tour. 1771*. Vol. IV, p. 361. As quoted in R. H. Tawney, *Equality*, p. 94.

INDEX

Abbott, Edith, 97; quoted, 97
Advisory Committee to the Commissioner of Social Security, 115
AFDC, 38, 40, 41, 53 n., 55, 82 n., 90, 100, 101, 103, 104, 105, 118, 122 n., 124, 171; and children without fathers, 18; and NEGIT, 133, 138; state-federal relationship in, 102
AFL-CIO, 149
age classifications, in income maintenance program, 64
Aid to Families with Dependent Children, *see* AFDC
American Marriage and Divorce, 118 n.
And the Poor Get Children, 44 n.
Annual Report of the Council of Economic Advisers, The, 12 n.
Australia, 115
automation, 50, 51, 59
"average need," and NEGIT, 130

Beveridge, William, 58, 114
Beveridge Report, 114
birth control, 78, 80
birth rate, 20, 21; early marriage related to, 77; and family allowances, 68–72, 83; of foreign countries, 67, 68–72; and housing policies, 76; and income maintenance programs, 67, 75, 82, 83, 84; income related to, 39, 65–84; long-term decline of, in U.S., 73, 74; and preschool allowance, 157; *see also* child-bearing; fertility
Blue Collar Marriage, 44 n.
blue-collar workers, 30
Brady, Dorothy, quoted, 89
Burns, Eveline, 57, 58, 98, 99, 130; quoted, 98, 99
Butler, Hugh, 131

Canada, 72, 82 n., 107, 148, 162; birth rate in, 68–70, 71; family allowance program in, 148; gross reproduction rate in, 1926–1962 (table), 175
"capital, social," 167
census (1960), 113
child-bearing, and initial marriage, 25–30, 37, 38, 42, 73, 82; *see also* birth rate; fertility
Children of Sanchez, The, 44 n.
Civil Rights Act (1964), 88

201

Index

collective bargaining, 161
Colorado, AFDC payments in, 102
Committee on Economic Security, President's, 3, 4, 15, 16, 96
contraception, 78, 80
Council of Economic Advisers, 89, 91
Culturally Deprived Child, The, 44 *n.*
cybernation, 50, 51, 59

Daedalus, 179 *n.*
Decisions about People in Need, 53 *n.*
demogrant, 6, 99
Denmark, 132, 162
Department of Agriculture, 89; economy food plan of, 12
Department of Labor, 62
Dépopulation et Civilization, 28 *n.*
diet: adequate, at low cost, 89; and inadequate income, 12
divorce, 20, 21, 43, 44, 114, 118 *n.*, 119, 124, 126
Douglas, Paul H., 54, 76, 148; quoted, 77
Dumont, Arsène, quoted, 28 *n.*
Dynamics of Bureaucracy, The, 53 *n.*

Economic Opportunity Act, 153
"economic tension" hypothesis, 37 *n.*
economy food plan, of Department of Agriculture, 12
education, 15, 32, 109; of husband, and occupation (table), 26; and income, 30; as "regulator" of fertility, 76
Education Act (1965), 153
Eighth Generation, The, 44 *n.*
Eldridge, Hope, quoted, 73–74, 110
employment, of women, 59–64
England, 66, 114, 158, 168; birth rate in, 67; public services in, 108
Erikson, Erik H., quoted, 35

family: breakdown of, 42–45; childless, 33; extreme types of, 34;
headed by woman, 17, 21, 137, 176; NEGIT payments to, proposed (table), 176; Negro, *see* Negro family; poor, in 1963, and number of children (table), 39; unable to move, 33 and *n.*; and working mother, 37
family allowance programs, 146–165, 179; and AFL-CIO, 149; birth rate affected by, 68–72, 83; in Canada, 148; cost of, 151, 153, 160; defined, 147; and marital stability, 157; by number of children, 146–147, 177, 178; proposal for, 151–155; *see also* preschool allowance
family cycle squeeze, 36–41, 156
family-income cycle, 23–48 *passim,* 80, 138–142; and "culture of poverty," 24; early marriage related to, 25–28; and family breakdown, 42–45; and NEGIT, 138–142; occupational choice related to, 30–36; *see also* family cycle squeeze
fatherless child insurance, 112–128, 140, 146, 155, 165; and child's portion, 125–126; coverage of, 117–121; defined, 113; financed by taxation, 127; and marital stability, 121, 123, 124–125; proposal for, 115–117; and take-off, 121–125
Fatherless Families, 114
Federal Old Age Survivors and Disability Insurance, 180
fertility, factors influencing, 73–83; *see also* birth rate; child-bearing
France, 83, 148, 162; birth rate in, 70, 71, 72
Freedman, Deborah, 74
Freedman, Ronald, 37 *n.,* 79
Friedman, Milton, 130

Galbraith, John, 168 *n.*
Germany, Nazi, 72
Glick, Paul, 27, 118 *n.*

202

203

There are an appalling 13.9 million children under fifteen who live in poverty in the United States. Citizens of a nation often called the most child-centered in the world, most of these children live in houses that lack a proper toilet, bath, or hot water.

What shall we do about them?

This book candidly — yet unsensationally — examines the poignant situation of poor children. In the light of their effects on family life, it also analyzes fatherless-child insurance, a negative income tax, family allowances, and the various other income maintenance programs that have been proposed as remedies.

Each of these programs, it becomes clear, has its peculiar advantages and drawbacks, and public policy, if it is to come to grips with the problem of children in poverty, will have to be far more imaginative and flexible than has hitherto been the case.